The Twilight Zone

TV Milestones Series

Series Editor
Barry Keith Grant, Brock University

A complete listing of the advisory editors and the books in this series can be found online at wsupress.wayne.edu

THE TWILIGHT ZONE

Barry Keith Grant

TV MILESTONES SERIES

Wayne State University Press Detroit

ISBN 978-0-8143-4578-8 (paperback)
ISBN 978-0-8143-4579-5 (e-book)

Library of Congress Control Number: 2019948555

Wayne State University Press
Leonard N. Simons Building
4809 Woodward Avenue
Detroit, Michigan 48201-1309

Visit us online at wsupress.wayne.edu

CONTENTS

ACKNOWLEDGMENTS

Many thanks to editor-in-chief Annie Martin and acquisitions editor Marie Sweetman at Wayne State University Press for their strong and continuing support, as well as to Kathy Wildfong and Carrie Downes Teefey for their excellent production work. Sal Borriello once again provided the careful copyediting. Jeannette Sloniowski and Joanne Morreale helped with research, as did Ian Gordon, librarian at Brock University. Rob Macmorine of the Department of Communications, Popular Culture, and Film at Brock University and Iain Stenhouse provided invaluable technical assistance. A special thank you to Dr. Ingrid Makus, Dean of Social Sciences at Brock, for her continuing support of my research. I am grateful to the three anonymous readers of the manuscript, whose thoughtful readings provided many helpful suggestions, all of which I've attempted to incorporate in revision.

Zoning In

Submitted—as *The Twilight Zone*'s creator, host, executive producer, and primary writer Rod Serling might have said—for your consideration: two televisual references (among many) to the original *The Twilight Zone*, one of the most memorable network-era television dramatic series of all time.*

The first reference: In an episode of the contemporary animated series *Family Guy* (Fox, 1998–) entitled "Wasted Talent," first aired July 5, 2000, Peter Griffin discovers he has the ability to play the piano only when drunk. When his wife, Lois, wonders about the extent to which alcohol is affecting his mental health, a zoom shot into Peter's cranium shows that all the brain cells have died because of his excessive drinking—except for one lone cell, who wears glasses (it is a brain cell, after all, even if it does belong to Peter Griffin). The brain cell's glasses fall off and shatter as it cries "It's not fair!" This, of course, is a reference to one of the best-remembered *Twilight Zone* episodes, "Time Enough at Last" (1.8: November 20, 1959), starring Burgess Meredith as misanthropic bank clerk Henry Bemis, a schnook

* Serling said "submitted for your consideration" when introducing two episodes, "The Trouble with Templeton" (2.9: December 9, 1960) and "To Serve Man," although the phrase has become associated with him.

who just wants to be left alone to read but who meets the same ironic fate as Peter's brain cell after an atomic war leaves him the only person alive.

The second reference, seventeen years later: On the evening broadcast of *The Late Show* on June 29, 2017, host Stephen Colbert—in what had become an almost-nightly ritual for him and other late-night-comedy-show hosts since the new president took office that January—once again skewered President Donald Trump. On this occasion, following Trump's attacks on Joe Scarborough and Mika Brzezinski of MSNBC's *Morning Joe*, Colbert showed a clip of Sarah Huckabee Sanders, then deputy press secretary, at a White House briefing saying that to be surprised to see the president on the attack after being criticized by these news anchors is like being "in the twilight zone." Colbert followed up by looking into the camera and declaring, "Oh, I love *The Twilight Zone*. Which one is he again? Is he the little boy with no morals who has the power to kill? 'Cause it's definitely not the guy who wants to be alone reading books." His joke about Trump's anti-intellectualism alludes to the same *Twilight Zone* episode as *The Family Guy* reference as well as another, "It's a Good Life" (3.8: November 3, 1961), about a family terrorized by a small boy (Billy Mumy) who can make anything happen just by thinking it and whose fates therefore hang always on his whims.

Both of these allusions assume not only that the audience will get the reference to a television show that was first broadcast more than half a century ago but also that they will know specific episodes. Such intense viewer appreciation of individual episodes, rather than merely of the show generally, is a distinctive feature of *Twilight Zone* fandom. This marked fan enthusiasm for the show also provides the joke that informs the opening of the film spinoff *Twilight Zone: The Movie* (1983). (Significantly, of the many television shows that have inspired movie adaptations, *The Twilight Zone* is the only anthology show—that is, one without recurring characters—to do so.

Burgess Meredith as the unfortunate Henry Bemis in "Time Enough at Last."

What viewers tend to remember from the show are issues and ideas—and, of course, the twist endings—more than characters.) *Twilight Zone: The Movie* featured new versions of three memorable episodes of the show—"Kick the Can" (3.21: February 9, 1962), "It's a Good Life," and "Nightmare at 20,000 Feet" (5.3: October 11, 1963)—as well as a new story, "Time Out," all preceded by a short prologue. Each of the episodes was done by a different director, each of whom already had been associated with fantastic cinema: John Landis, Steven Spielberg, Joe Dante, George Miller. In the prologue, also directed by Landis, two nameless guys (Dan Ackroyd, Albert Brooks) are driving through the vast American southwest in the dark of night. To pass the time, they begin to play trivia, at first challenging each other to identify television-show theme songs. Inevitably, they come around to French composer Marius Constant's distinctive theme for *The Twilight Zone*—probably the most instantly recognizable television theme music of all time—and, discovering a shared love for the show, they then take turns recalling some of their favorite episodes ("Remember the one where . . . ?"), repeating a conversation already had innumerable times by baby boomers everywhere (including, I confess, the author of this book).

Of course, their trivia game can only be topped by a twist worthy of *The Twilight Zone* itself. Ackroyd asks Brooks if he wants to see something "really scary," to which Brooks cautiously agrees. Then Ackroyd turns into a quickly glimpsed hideous monster who, as the film cuts to a long shot outside the car, is heard chomping on the unfortunate Brooks before the camera tilts up into the nighttime sky to evoke the familiar opening and closing shots of the television show's stories—narrated now by none other than Burgess Meredith (who, while best remembered for "Time Enough at Last," starred in three other *Twilight Zone* episodes as well).

The Twilight Zone ran on CBS for five seasons, from October 1959 to June 1964. During its run, the show was nominated for multiple awards, winning three Emmys (two for Serling as writer and one for George T. Clemens for Outstanding Achievement in Cinematography for Television) as well as a Golden Globe Award for Serling for Best Producer/Director. For each of its first three seasons it won a Hugo Award from the World Science Fiction Society for Best Dramatic Achievement. On the show's coattails the network launched a similar series, *'Way Out*, in 1961, hosted by offbeat writer Roald Dahl, to pair with *The Twilight Zone* on Friday evenings, while ABC "countered" with *The Outer Limits* (ABC, 1963–65).

The show has continuously been in reruns on American television, and all of the original 156 episodes (with a handful of exceptions) are available on streaming services such as Hulu and iTunes. The Syfy channel has programmed a *Twilight Zone* marathon on New Year's Eve for two decades. CBS's website offers ten episodes for free and the others by subscription.

In the age of the internet, there are numerous websites devoted exclusively or in part to the show or to Rod Serling.

In first run, *The Twilight Zone*'s ratings were never very strong. "We were always on the verge of getting canceled," recalled producer Buck Houghton (Grams, 67). It was pitted first against *77 Sunset Strip* (1958–64) on ABC and then *The Detectives* (ABC, 1959–61; NBC, 1961–62) with Robert Taylor and NBC's reliable *Gillette Cavalcade of Sports* (1946–60). But by the midpoint of the first season of thirty-six episodes, the show's ratings improved somewhat, and the network realized it had a "prestige program" (King, 232). The critics were generally enthusiastic: Cecil Smith of the *Los Angeles Times* called it "the finest weekly series of the season," while John Crosby of the *New York Herald Tribune* said it was "certainly the best and most original anthology series of the year" (qtd. in Presnell and McGee, 16). Terry Turner of the *Chicago Daily News* wrote that *The Twilight Zone* "is about the only show now on the air that I actually look forward to seeing. It's the one series that I will let interfere with other plans" (Zicree, 96–97). While its audience share may not have been exceptionally large, the viewership it did generate was exceptionally loyal—"all over America on Friday nights people held *Twilight Zone* parties" (Zicree, 211)—and it is no surprise that *TV Guide* ranked the show eighth in its list of the "25 Top Cult shows Ever!" (May 30, 2004). Yet despite its critical success, each season the show seemed to hang on, finding sponsors at the eleventh hour until, finally, after five years, James Aubrey, vice-president of CBS in charge of programming and then president during *The Twilight Zone*'s run, finally canceled it, citing cost overruns, relatively tepid ratings, and the skittishness of sponsors (Murray).

Since then, the continuing popularity of the show is clear from the numerous transmedia iterations and references to it that, as already suggested, have appeared across the many forms of popular culture, as a quick survey reveals. In print, while the show was still in first run Serling novelized several of his original scripts for the anthologies *Stories from the Twilight Zone* (1960), *More Stories from the Twilight Zone* (1961), and *New Stories from the Twilight Zone* (1962), all of which have enjoyed multiple printings and together have sold millions of copies, as has *The Twilight Zone: Complete Stories*, published in 1980. In 1995, DAW Books, a science-fiction and fantasy imprint, published three anthologies edited by Serling's widow, Carol Serling—*Journeys to the Twilight Zone*, *Return to the Twilight Zone*, and *Adventures in the Twilight Zone*—each of which contained a story by Rod Serling. Gauntlet Press in Colorado completed a ten-volume set of original scripts from *The Twilight Zone* by Serling in 2013, as well as books of scripts by the show's two most frequent writers after Serling, Charles Beaumont and Richard Matheson. In September 2009, Tor Books published *Twilight Zone: 19 Original Stories on the 50th Anniversary*, containing new tales by contemporary authors such as R. L. Stine, to mark the fiftieth anniversary of the show. There also have been several comic book tie-ins, including one from Gold Key (Western Publishing) that ran ninety-one issues from 1963 to 1979, and *The Twilight Zone Magazine* (also known as *Rod Serling's Twilight Zone Magazine*), which was published monthly from 1981 to 1989.

Musical artists representing a wide diversity of styles have created work based on *The Twilight Zone*, among them John Cale, Iron Maiden, Manhattan Transfer, the Ventures, and the Residents. Contemporaneously with the show, in 1964 a Los Angeles session group named the Marketts had a number 3 charted hit, "Out of Limits," which clearly echoed the show's theme music. Episodes of the show have been adapted for radio broadcast on both subscription and commercial radio, with Stacy Keach replacing Serling as narrator. The script for the episode "The Monsters Are Due on Maple Street" (1.22: March 4, 1960), one of the most famous, has been published as a play for student production, and live theater productions of original episodes have been staged in several cities, including

Los Angeles, London, and Seattle, where Theater Schmeater has mounted a continuing show, "The Twilight Zone—Live," with permission of the Serling estate, since 1996. Also based on the series, The Twilight Zone Tower of Terror is an attraction at several Disney theme parks (the one at Disney California Adventure Park in Anaheim was closed in 2017). The show was adapted as a board game by Ideal in 1964, during its initial run, and as a video game in 1988 and a pinball game by Bally in 1992.

The show has been parodied many times. One of the earliest, on *The Jack Benny Program* (CBS, 1950–64, NBC, 1964–65) broadcast on January 15, 1963, begins with Benny hiring Serling to help improve the level of writing on his show. Their meeting falls apart when Serling confesses that he doesn't understand Benny's comedy and Benny admits that *The Twilight Zone* never really made any sense to him. On his way home Benny, lost in a thick fog, notices a signpost up ahead indicating that he is in the Twilight Zone ("subconscious" twenty-seven miles ahead, "reality" twenty-five miles behind). He manages to find his house, but Eddie "Rochester" Anderson, who plays Benny's servant on his show, doesn't recognize him when he gets there. Serling, now owner of the house and mayor of the town, appears in a dressing gown and, exploiting a running joke about Benny's age, observes that "anyone who claims to be thirty-nine years old for as long as he has is a permanent resident of the Twilight Zone."

Since its initial run, many of the show's "plots, characters, and conceits entered the American consciousness . . . supplying a rich bank of iconic images" (Norris, 3–4). Thus, it is no surprise that, according to Serling biographer Joel Engel, the volume and variety of merchandising made *The Twilight Zone* "one of the most profitable shows in the history of television" (235). The mountain of merchandising it has generated includes a face mask of the gremlin on the airplane wing in the "Nightmare at 20,000 Feet" episode, a decal of the open door in the later series opening, and a replica of the tabletop fortune-telling machine from the episode "The Nick of Time" (2.7: November 18, 1960). There are the inevitable coffee mugs and action figures of many of the characters, such as the robot Alicia from "The Lonely" (1.7: November 15, 1959) (with her humanoid face ripped off, of course, as in the climax of the episode), a nurse and doctor from "Eye of the Beholder" (2.6: November 11, 1960), various aliens such as the three-eyed soda jerk from "Will the Real Martian Please Stand Up?" (2.28: May 26, 1961), and (ironically) Jerry and the evil Willie from "The Dummy" (3.33: May 4, 1962). One can purchase black T-shirts with the show's name in its distinctive angular font or with other variations from the CBS store. The wittiest T-shirt available, I think, is one referencing the episode "To Serve Man" (3.24: March 2, 1962), in which it is discovered that human tourists flocking to the home world of the alien Kanamits actually are being cooked and eaten; the shirt features the face of a Kanamit dressed as Colonel Sanders with the logo "KFH" (presumably, Kanamit Fried Human) and slogan "Looking Forward to Serving You."

The Twilight Zone has been revived thrice: first on CBS for two seasons from 1985–87, with actor Charles Aidman as host (Aidman had starred in two episodes of the original series, "And When the Sky Was Opened" [1.11: December 11, 1959] and "Little Girl Lost" [3.26: March 16, 1962]) and running for sixty-five episodes; in 2002–2003 for one season on UPN, with Forest Whitaker as host and lasting for forty-three episodes; and most recently, on CBS All Access beginning in April, 2019, with Jordan Peele as host. The UPN iteration included remakes of some original classic episodes, such as "Eye of the Beholder" and "The Monsters Are Due on Maple Street," as well as "It's Still a Good Life," a sequel to "It's a Good Life" with Billy Mumy returning to the role of the monstrous child Anthony now as an adult. In the newest version, Jordan Peele (who also acts as executive producer) may at first seem an unlikely choice to serve as host given his association with comedy (earlier in his career he appeared for five seasons on *Mad TV* [Fox, 1995–2000; CW,

2016–] and with Keegan-Michael Key for three years on *Key & Peele* [Comedy Central, 2012–15]); but clearly he hopes to build on the success of his award-winning horror/comedy *Get Out* (2017). Peele has acknowledged that his subsequent feature film, *Us* (2019), released just before the launch of his *Twilight Zone* reboot, was inspired in part by the original *Twilight Zone* episode "Mirror Image" (1.21: February 26, 1960), further reinforcing his association with horror rather than comedy and his fit as host of the new show. While some of the episodes of Peele's version may be more overtly political, none of these hosts come close to attaining anything like the remarkable resonance, as discussed in chapter 2, of Rod Serling.

Later shows that are commonly seen as having been influenced by *The Twilight Zone* include *The X-Files* (Fox, 1993–2002, 2016–) and *Black Mirror* (Channel 4, 2011–14; Netflix, 2016–). One of the latter show's most highly regarded episodes, "San Junipero" (third series, 2016), was inspired by the premises of the *Twilight Zone* episodes "Walking Distance" (1.5: October 30, 1959) and "A Stop at Willoughby" (1.30: May 6, 1960). The show also has influenced many feature films, providing them with similarly speculative premises. A partial list includes *Liar, Liar* (1997), about a man who is cursed to tell the truth (2.14: "The Whole Truth" [February 20, 1961]); *Child's Play* (1988), about a killer doll (5.6: "Living Doll" [November 1, 1963]); *Frequency* (2001), involving a radio that broadcasts transmissions from the past (2.20: "Static" [March 10, 1961]); *Real Steel* (2011), about boxing robots (5.2: "Steel" [October 4, 1963]); *Time Lapse* (2014), about a camera that takes pictures of the future (2.10: "A Most Unusual Camera" [December 16, 1960]); *The Truman Show* (1998), about a man who discovers that his life is an arranged reality-television show (1.23: "A World of Difference" [March 11, 1960]); and *Her* (2013), about a lonely man who falls in love with his computer's operating system ("The Lonely"). One might even consider *Poltergeist* (1982) to have been inspired in part by the episode "Little Girl Lost" and the family-friendly *Toy Story* (1995) by the Pirandellian episode "Five Characters in Search of an Exit" (3.14: December 22, 1961), which tells the story of a group of dolls in a Christmas donation bin wondering who and where they are. Several of M. Night Shyamalan's films, including *The Sixth Sense* (1999), *Signs* (2002), *The Village* (2004), and *The Visit* (2015), as well as similar fantastic films like the Duffer brothers' *Hidden* (2015), involve twist endings that are clearly indebted to the show. *Devil* (2010), based on a story by Shyamalan, places Satan disguised as a human among a group of people trapped in an elevator, much like the similarly disguised Martian in the snowbound diner in "Will the Real Martian Please Stand Up?"

Even today, most North Americans, including those born after the show's initial run, know the series' distinctive theme music, the first few notes of which have come to represent an iconographic shorthand for something odd or weird occurring. The theme music for the first season was provided by Bernard Herrmann, the distinguished Hollywood composer who had a long association with Alfred Hitchcock, but it was changed toward the end of the season to Marius Constant's more familiar theme. Constant had been commissioned by Lud Gluskin, director of music for CBS, to provide some short pieces for the company's stock library. He created the *Twilight Zone* theme by editing two of them together (Grams, 70–72), one featuring those opening four repeated notes on electric guitar (played by jazz guitarist Howard Roberts). The bongos toward the end add a hint of bohemian weirdness appropriate to the show's fantastic ambiance.

This lengthy catalog of the show's cultural afterlife makes clear the astonishing popularity *The Twilight Zone* has had and that shows no sign of abating more than half a century after it was on the air. This cultural impact alone guarantees its "enduring status" (Murray) as a television milestone. But the show is also important as a prism through which to see the turbulence roiling within contemporary American culture. During its run, the show spanned the seismic transition from the 1950s to the 1960s—in the words of Stephen King, "From the torpor of the Eisenhower administration to LBJ's escalation of American involvement in Vietnam, the first of the long hot summers in American cities, and the advent of the Beatles" (King, 229). In those mere five years, the Cold War heated up to boiling point when American and Soviet tanks faced each other in August 1961 as construction began on the Berlin Wall and then during the Cuban Missile Crisis in October the following year. Nuclear tests by both countries proliferated in the decade, and, beginning with a hydrogen-bomb detonation at the Nevada proving grounds in July 1962, the US began testing within its own borders. Communist China detonated its first atomic bomb in 1964, joining the ranks of the superpowers. People were busy buying and building fallout shelters, and "duck and cover" drills continued to be practiced in the nation's public schools when *Twilight Zone* episodes invoking the horrors of atomic warfare such as "Time Enough at Last," "Third from the Sun" (1.14: January 8, 1960), and "The Shelter" (3.3: September 29, 1961) were being broadcast across the nation. The show's stories, and the characters in them experiencing trauma of one form or another week after week, artfully revealed the stresses at work within American society as well as what Alvin Toffler called "future shock," the accelerating rate of technological and social change and its psychological effects upon people.

At home, American society fragmented as the various challenges to state power were met with increasing and sometimes violent resistance. While some progress was made in civil rights, in June 1963 Alabama governor George Wallace personally blocked the entrance to the University of Alabama in Tuscaloosa when the first two black students, escorted by federal troops, arrived to register. A year later three white civil-rights workers were arrested and then murdered in Philadelphia, Mississippi. Soon black militancy would arise with the Black

Panthers, although by the end of the decade most of that group's leaders were either in jail or dead. In 1964, the year *The Twilight Zone* concluded its five-season run, Bob Dylan diagnosed the state of American culture when he sang "The Times They Are A-Changin'," noting that "there's a battle outside and it's ragin'."

The show also bridged the significant cultural transition of the fantastic genres—science fiction, horror, and fantasy—from marginal to mainstream, from being scorned as subliterature to embraced as serious art. When *The Twilight Zone* began, these genres, apart from a few canonical exceptions (Edgar Allan Poe, H. G. Wells, Mary Shelley, Aldous Huxley, George Orwell), were mostly dismissed by cultural critics and tastemakers. By the time the show left the airwaves, Ray Bradbury's *Fahrenheit 451* (1953), J. R. R. Tolkien's *Lord of the Rings* (1954–55), Robert Heinlein's *Stranger in a Strange Land* (1961), and Kurt Vonnegut's early works *Player Piano* (1952), *The Sirens of Titan* (1959), and *Cat's Cradle* (1963) were becoming countercultural cult novels. By decade's end these and other science-fiction books were beginning to appear in undergraduate English course syllabi across the country.

In film, shortly before *The Twilight Zone* premiered, science fiction typically translated the anxieties of the atomic era into B-movie creature features. Men mutated into monsters in such movies as *The Amazing Colossal Man* (1957) and *The Beast of Yucca Flats* (1961), while creatures of every kind took wing and tunneled, crawled, and climbed their way through similar plots featuring scenes of mass destruction, fleeing citizens, and the deployment of military personnel and hardware. This monstrous menagerie included giant ants (*Them!* [1954]), arachnids (*Tarantula* [1955]), grasshoppers (*Beginning of the End* [1957]), octopi (*It Came from beneath the Sea* [1955]), and crustacea (*Attack of the Crab Monsters* [1957]). Usually, these creatures were explained as mutations accidentally generated by atomic testing or ancient slumbering beasts awakened by them—more hyberbolic in their metaphors than *The Twilight Zone* but borne of shared anxieties and fears.

Hitchcock's *Psycho* (1960), released six months after *The Twilight Zone* debuted, utterly transformed the genre of the horror film by situating its monster, a serial killer with the appearance and charm of the boy next door, emphatically within the normal and the commonplace rather than an exoticized elsewhere like the Transylvania of *Dracula* (1931), the uncharted *Island of Lost Souls* (1932), or the West Indian jungle of *I Walked with a Zombie* (1943). In contrast to such movies, *Psycho*'s settings include a cheap hotel room, mundane real-estate office, used-car lot, and a nondescript motel (including a bathroom with toilet!)—the kind of banal places frequently seen in *The Twilight Zone*, such as a typical bus depot ("Mirror Image"), roadside diner ("Will the Real Martian Please Stand Up?"), and, too, cheap hotel room ("A Most Unusual Camera") and used-car lot ("The Whole Truth"). *The Twilight Zone* certainly had its futuristic settings and alien worlds, but these were less common than the commonplace—even when the world is otherworldly, as in such episodes as "Third from the Sun," "People Are Alike All Over" (1.25: March 25, 1960), and "Elegy" (1.20: February 19, 1960). Indeed, for philosopher Mary Sirridge, the show offers nothing less than a warning about what she calls "the treachery of the commonplace" (Sirridge, 58–76). Paradoxically, *The Twilight Zone* explored the fringes of the fantastic but remained fixed in the familiar, and, like Hitchcock's film, it revealed the monstrous within the normal and explored how thin the veneer of civilization in fact is.

Other movies such as Stanley Kramer's *On the Beach* (1959), Hitchcock's *The Birds* (1963), and Stanley Kubrick's *Dr. Strangelove or: How I Learned to Stop Worrying and Love the Bomb* (1964) showed established auteurs turning to science fiction and horror, a trend that culminated toward the end of the decade with *2001: A Space Odyssey* (1968), regarded by many as a masterwork of philosophical cinema and the greatest science-fiction film ever made. Bridging this rise to respectability for horror, science fiction, and fantasy, *The Twilight Zone* was at the same time responsible for much of the dramatic and pronounced cultural shift in attitude.

Unsurprisingly, there has been a great deal already written about *The Twilight Zone*—indeed, there is perhaps as much scholarly and fan writing about it as for any other show in television history. Writers have looked at the show from a panoply of perspectives, examining its production history, its style, its politics, the trivia. There are at least three books (Zicree, Presnell and McGee, Grams) that offer commentaries on every episode. The show has been discussed in the historical context of its changing representation of the frontier (Norris), its use of cultural myth (Hill), its response to technological change (Laudadio), even as a precursor of postmodernism (Booker). In this book, though, my focus is primarily on the interrelated questions of authorship, genre, style, and ideology in the context of *The Twilight Zone*. The on- and off-screen influence of executive producer and writer Rod Serling, the show's unique and complex approach to genre, and the anxieties of the age all came together to make it the memorable show it was.

A short volume such as this one might well have focused primarily on, say, important issues of representation involving race or gender—issues that have been of considerable interest to scholars, to be sure. However, I have chosen not to make them my primary focus here, as one doesn't have to look too deeply to see that *The Twilight Zone* is rooted in a white male perspective. Most obviously, the makers of the show were almost entirely white men, as are the overwhelming majority of the show's protagonists. Only one episode was directed by a woman ("The Masks" [5.25: March 20, 1964], by Ida Lupino), and only one was written by a woman ("Caesar and Me" [5.28: April 10, 1964], by A. T. Strassfield). Although a few episodes do offer female protagonists—Helen Foley (Janice Rule), for example, in "Nightmare as a Child" (1.29: April 29,

1960) or Marsha White (Anne Francis) in "The After Hours" (1.34: June 10, 1960)—more often they were conceived and performed as stereotypes, frequently as harridans constraining men. Gart Williams's entirely unsympathetic wife, Jane (Patricia Donahue), in "A Stop at Willoughby," who seems to care only for material comfort and nothing for her husband, is only the most strident of the lot.

In "The Chaser" (1.31: May 13, 1960), Roger Shackleforth (George Grizzard) gives a love potion to Leila (Patricia Barry), the shallow woman he loves but who cares nothing for him; predictably, she becomes a cloying, doting wife who smothers him with her devotion. We learn nothing about how Leila might feel about her bewitchment: the episode, like most, is resolutely positioned within the masculine perspective—Roger's story and not Leila's. In "A Penny for Your Thoughts" (2.16: February 3, 1961), when bank clerk Hector B. Poole (Dick York), who has gained the ability to read the mind of whoever is in physical proximity, walks past the people in the bank, the soundtrack features an audio montage of their thoughts, but when he gets to the blonde fondling a wad of cash there is a resounding silence on the soundtrack—a tired "dumb blonde" joke that represents the show's attitude toward women at its worst. Serling was possibly aware of the show's disproportional gender representation because among the changes to the series he promised in the second season was that there would be more female protagonists (Grams, 90), although the show's masculine bias never really did change.

Certainly, one might read the overwhelming majority of the show's episodes as being about what scholars would identify as revealing masculinity in crisis. In addition to several episodes that reveal men beleaguered if not emasculated by their wives, others such as "The Bewitchin' Pool" (June 19, 1964) reveal married couples locked in mutual hatred and recrimination. The most recurrent image in the show is that of a close-up of a man's face, sweaty and emotionally overwrought, as he experiences a psychic breakdown of some sort in the dramatic climax. But such an analysis hardly requires reading against the grain to elucidate it.

Visible minorities appeared infrequently on the show, as was the case for all of network television at the time, and on the few occasions when they did, like the simple Mexican peasants of "Dust" (2.12: January 6, 1961) and "The Gift" (3.32: April 27, 1962), they were little more than stereotypes. While Serling did call out network television for omitting black actors from the small screen (Zicree, 112) and boldly cast black actors in the episode "The Big Tall Wish" (1.27: April 8, 1960), it is also the case that only white people are shown living on Maple Street and in Willoughby. One of the reasons Serling shifted his efforts from writing prestige television dramas for shows such as *Playhouse 90* (CBS, 1958–60) and *Kraft Television Theatre* (NBC, 1947–58) to a lowbrow fantasy and science-fiction series was to avoid the kind of overt and heavy-handed censorship he had experienced when attempting to address matters of race on television.

According to Lester H. Hunt, the turning point in Serling's approach as a writer from a realist treatment of social issues based on actual events to a more fantastic mode in which the critiques were more generalized was his experience involving his script "Noon on Doomsday" for the *United States Steel Hour* (ABC, 1953–55; CBS, 1955–63), broadcast on April 25, 1956 (12–22). The plot was originally based on the notorious murder of Emmett Till, a black teenager from Chicago who was killed by two white men for whistling at a white woman in Mississippi where he was visiting family. The two men charged with the murder were acquitted, as was the killer in Serling's script. US Steel, nervous about the racial connection, relocated the town to New England, changed the victim from Jewish to a vaguely identified foreigner, and eliminated any references to lynching, so that, according to Marc Scott Zicree, "When it was finally aired in April of 1956, 'Noon on Doomsday' was so watered down as to be meaningless" (14).

Two years later Serling wrote another script ("especially written," according to the closing credits) on a similar topic, "A Town Has Turned to Dust," for *Playhouse 90*. Although Serling later said that the sponsors and studio execs "chopped it up like a roomful of butchers at work on a steer" (Zicree, 15) and that "a script had turned to dust," Hunt rightly finds the drama, which was directed by John Frankenheimer, "as powerful and focused as that of 'Noon' is weak and vague" (19) because Serling recast the story as a Western. Many of the dramatic techniques that Serling would bring to *The Twilight Zone* are already present in "A Town Has Turned to Dust," including the use of a newspaper reporter (James Gregory) who provides commentary periodically and at the end and who explicitly drives home the point that the story provides "a lesson that must be learned by all men."

The firm, familiar frameworks of generic tradition allowed Serling greater potential to offer social criticism in his work, although, as we shall see, the politics of *The Twilight Zone* were ultimately contradictory, at once both critical and conservative, this very tension helping to make *The Twilight Zone* so important and memorable. In what follows, I focus on the place of *The Twilight Zone* within the various modes of the fantastic, showing how it combined them with other generic traditions to offer social criticism cast as moral fables. As I explain, the show offered a complex mix of generic codes and conventions that provided a shared visual shorthand to viewers that helped make its messages more acceptable to a mainstream prime-time audience. Television scholar Jason Mittell has argued for an understanding of genres in the medium not as text based but "as a process of categorization" that "operates across the cultural realms of media industries, audiences, policy, critics, and historical contexts" (2004, xii). *The Twilight Zone* serves as a case in point, as it was the fantasy nature of the show, regarded primarily as lowbrow material for juvenile audiences, that allowed Serling to offer his brand of social criticism. "A Martian," he once declared, "can say things that a Republican or Democrat can't" (qtd. in Javna, 16).

I then examine the singular case of authorship of *The Twilight Zone*. As executive producer, chief writer, and on-screen host, Serling was indisputably the main creative force of the show, but how did this authorial control function when numerous established directors, writers, actors, and others were also involved in the show's production? In examining his vision in *The Twilight Zone* and in his other work, I show how Serling provided the artistic vision of the series, in effect as one of television's first showrunners—possibly the first, well before that term even existed. Tracing motifs and themes in the show, I consider how it functioned as an ideal instance of collective authorship built around Serling's concern with questions of individual morality and democratic principles.

In the final chapter I examine the politics of the show, how it responded to both national and world events and how these related to Serling's moral vision as it was expressed in individual episodes and across the series' run. Of course, the ideological values expressed by *The Twilight Zone*, whether deliberately or not, are inextricable from a consideration of Serling's authorial voice; I separate them here only for the sake of discussion. Serling was a moralist writing for a mass medium in a rapidly changing society during the height of the Cold War, and the conflicting and conflicted messages of the show's various episodes inevitably express not only the political tensions of the time but also the commercial nature of television as a form of cultural production. The frequent narrative tensions in the series between art and commerce, individualism and conformity, and nostalgia and modernism express Serling's conflicted view of television as a medium, and they also may be understood as paradigmatic of that moment in television history when the so-called Golden Age of live television drama was pivoting toward more formula-driven filmed series.

My aim throughout has been to offer the most productive and comprehensive account of *The Twilight Zone* possible within the scope of a short volume. My approach and organization allow me to discuss the most important forces that shaped the show and the most salient concepts for understanding them. I also have sought to balance detailed analysis of a few selected episodes with broader discussions of multiple episodes in order to provide the necessary depth and breadth that any serious consideration of *The Twilight Zone*, a show that had no recurrent characters or plot premises, requires.

In a famous speech before the National Association of Broadcasters on May 9, 1961—about midway through *The Twilight Zone's* original run—Newton Minow, chairman of the Federal Communications Commission, attacked the television industry as "a vast wasteland." Referring to television's failure to grapple with real issues and problems, Minow's comments proved prophetic indeed as the decade unfolded. During the early 1960s popular network sitcoms like *The Andy Griffith Show* (CBS, 1960–68), *Car 54, Where Are You?* (NBC, 1961–63), *The Beverly Hillbillies* (CBS, 1962–71), *My Favorite Martian* (CBS, 1963–66), *The Munsters* (CBS, 1964–66), and *Gomer Pyle, U.S.M.C.* (CBS, 1964–69) presented escapist visions of an impossible America untroubled by the actual conflicts within contemporary society. Watching a show like *Green Acres* (CBS, 1965–71), with its bucolic depiction of a harmonious but clearly fantastic rural America, one would never know that political tensions including the war in Vietnam and civil-rights struggles were then rending the social fabric of the nation. The concurrent *Hogan's Heroes* (CBS, 1965–71) seemed to erase history entirely with its portrayal of funny and incompetent German soldiers running a World War II POW camp containing irrepressible American GIs. (Serling said that the only people who could appreciate it were those "who refuse to let history get in the way of their laughter" [qtd. in Murray]).

The most popular dramatic genre on television early on in the decade, the Western, also occasionally addressed social issues such as violence and racism but typically displaced them through the genre's iconography to a past already seemingly remote in the age of television and left them there. No twist ending or host drove home the story's relevance to the television audience in these shows. Tending to side with the moral righteousness of an unproblematic hero, most (but not all!) TV Westerns offered viewers an easy and comforting distinction between a more primitive (but necessary) stage of social evolution and our more happily enlightened present, where we know better. The early *Twilight Zone* episode "Execution" (1.26: April 1, 1960) addressed this point directly. In the story, Joe Caswell (Albert Salmi), an outlaw from the Wild West about to be hanged, is transported by time machine to the contemporary laboratory of Professor Manion (Russell Johnson). The brutish Caswell kills the scientist but is then overwhelmed by the bustle and noise of the modern city and so returns to the lab, where he in turn is killed by a burglar. The burglar then by chance transports himself back in time and ends up in the noose intended for Caswell. In addition to the show's frequently sardonic take on fate and justice, the episode suggests that modern man is no less corrupt and violent than he was in the past.

The Untouchables (ABC, 1959–63) and *Bonanza* (NBC, 1959–73), two enormously popular shows that premiered in the same season as *The Twilight Zone*, were rooted in America's mythic past. By contrast, while *The Twilight Zone* did feature some episodes set in the past—as well as in imagined futures—the show was emphatically rooted in the America of its time, responding to contemporary events as well as ruminating on the darker, more uncomfortable aspects of human nature and such Big Questions as faith, death, and mortality. If the later *Star Trek* (1966–69) envisioned an enlightened and lofty future in which humanity's current social problems have been solved, *The Twilight Zone* commonly cast its characters, and sometimes its viewers as well, into the "pit of man's fears." It was, for Newton Minow, one of the exceptions to the vast wasteland.

1
"Once Upon a Time"

The Twilight Zone *and Genre*

As the show's "look" makes clear, the makers of *The Twilight Zone* were quite aware of classic Hollywood styles and forms. In a close analysis of three representative episodes—"Time Enough at Last," "The Monsters Are Due on Maple Street," and "Nightmare at 20,000 Feet"—film scholar J. P. Telotte demonstrates that the show exhibits a surprisingly "cinematic nature" (2), mobilizing a sophisticated use of the gaze as it is constructed in film for narrative purposes and the ways those "cinematic possibilities might be used" in broadcast television (15). But if *The Twilight Zone* was "cinematic" and popular cinema is conceived, produced, and organized largely within generic parameters (see Grant 2007, 7–9), then in what genre or genres does the show fit? Was it science fiction? Fantasy? Horror? Thriller? And why does it matter? As we shall see, the show tapped into all of these genres and others as well, creating complex generic hybrids to make its dramatic points more effectively in the tight arc of the half-hour series format.

Some critics have noted the show's generic hybridity, but beyond such generalized observations no one has considered in detail how these mixed generic signifiers actually worked in the show. *TV Guide* in 1959 labeled *The Twilight Zone* with the vague descriptor "drama," avoiding any finer generic distinctions. In the early days of television criticism, Horace Newcomb categorized *The Twilight Zone* as science fiction, which he considered as one of several forms of the adventure genre (Newcomb). More recently, Lorna Jowett and Stacey Abbott place the show as horror in their book *TV Horror*. One critic describes the show as overlapping "into magic realism, poetic realism, fantasy, and comedy" (Norris, 6), while yet another argues for it as a modern version of Menippean satire (Booker), a traditional literary form represented by, for example, Petronius, Swift, and Voltaire. Aiming for inclusivity, Wikipedia today describes the show as "science-fiction, fantasy, psychological-supernatural horror."

The stories were set in a shadowy place called the "Twilight Zone," less a geographical location than a narrative space where anything could happen. "Couldn't happen, you say? Probably not in most places—but it did happen in the Twilight Zone," observes Serling at the end of the early episode "One for the Angels" (1.2: October 9, 1959), a view reiterated by the Professor (Robert Emhardt) in "Static," who replies to Ed's claim of hearing old broadcasts on his antique radio by cautioning, "Impossible? That's a dangerous sort of word to use nowadays." In "A Game of Pool" (3.5: October 13, 1961) Fats Brown (Jonathan Winters) tells wannabe champion Jesse Cardiff (Jack Klugman) that nothing is impossible, some things are only less likely than others. Each week in the first season, Serling's opening voice-over, following the theme music, described the "Twilight Zone" as "a fifth dimension, beyond that which is known to man . . . as vast as space and as timeless as infinity. It is the middle ground between light and shadow, between science and superstition. And it lies between the pit of man's fears and the summit of his knowledge." This vague and unbounded location was at once "too incredible to be real, too real to be a dream," as Serling describes it in the opening of the episode "In His Image" (4.1: January 3, 1963).

"The middle ground between light and shadow": the first-season opening.

Serling was well aware of the generic formulas at work in network television and employed them for his own purposes in *The Twilight Zone*. In an article he penned for the November 7, 1959, issue of *TV Guide* explaining why he committed himself to *The Twilight Zone*, he wrote, "When *Gunsmoke* [CBS, 1955–75] corrals an audience, the next season will see a herd of imitators varying in title and star but painfully similar. Peter Gunn goes off on a caper, and the next season fourteen other actors take out private-eye licenses, and the television audience is exposed to a diet of sameness that makes dial-switching superfluous" (Grams, 68). (In "Static" Ed Lindsay [Dean Jagger] scorns all the other seniors in the rooming house for spending their evenings watching formula television shows like the Western "Gunfire" that turn their brains into "oatmeal.") In the article Serling then offers *The Twilight Zone* as a contrast to this pattern of generic cycling and sameness.

Even as it mocked genre television, *The Twilight Zone* embraced genre iconography and convention for its own purposes. For example, the familiar elements of the Western—the American genre par excellence (Bazin, 141), toward the end of its glorious postwar flowering when *The Twilight Zone* began and dominating prime-time television at the time—appear in at least seven episodes, including "A Hundred Yards over the Rim" (2.23: April 7, 1961), "Mr. Garrity and the Graves" (5.32: May 8, 1964), and the aforementioned "Dust" and "Execution." In the comic "Showdown with Rance McGrew" (3.20: February 2, 1962) television cowboy star McGrew (Larry Blyden) finds himself suddenly transported back in time from a saloon set, where he is about to be shot in the back by a dastardly thespian Jesse James, to the actual Old West. The "real" Jesse James (Arch Johnson) explains the collective annoyance he and other famous outlaws are feeling because of the unflattering way they have been portrayed on his show. He returns to the present with McGrew, serving as a script advisor to make sure that the gunfighters of history are represented more positively in the future. Apart from its relevance today to a discussion of cultural representation and political correctness, the episode has an obvious "problem," which Zicree notes: "The 'real' Old West . . . is every bit as TV-phony as the bogus Old West in the episode. The sets are identical and the look is the same" (269). One might argue, as M. Keith Booker does for the show, that this is a postmodernist gesture on the part of the episode, for we were already willing to suspend our disbelief and regard the opening action as "real" until McGrew loudly arrives late, driving down Main Street kicking up the dust in the street with the tires of his Cadillac on what is now revealed to be a set. But certainly, it underscores the show's unwavering commitment to the shorthand of genre conventions to make its dramatic points.

Thus, for example, in the episode "The Four of Us Are Dying" (1.13: January 1, 1960) Arch Hammer (Harry Townes), who can change his face at will to take on the appearance of

Rance McGrew (Larry Blyden) drives into town in his Cadillac in "Showdown with Rance McGrew."

someone else, "assumes a series of identities (a trumpet player, a gangster, a boxer) that reads like a roll call of typical film noir characters" (Booker, 55). Similarly, in "Shadow Play" (2.26: May 5, 1961) Adam Grant (Dennis Weaver), who insists he is dreaming the world in which he is about to be executed for murder, explains twice—correctly—that the stereotyped characters and melodramatic look of the jail and execution chamber have been conjured from some bad movies he has seen. "A Nice Place to Visit" (1.28: April 15, 1960) features Larry Blyden as Rocky Valentine, a two-bit gangster who is depicted with all the conventions of the gangster film, including loud clothes and molls draped over his arms. Zicree criticizes Blyden's performance as "a third-rate composite impression of James Cagney, Edward G. Robinson, and George Raft" (114)—quite to the point for an intended warning that bad life decisions will doom you to dwell for eternity in "the other place."

"Mr. Denton on Doomsday" (1.3: October 16, 1959) illustrates how *The Twilight Zone* uses genre to deliberate effect. The episode stars Dan Duryea (an actor who had appeared earlier in several Westerns including Anthony Mann's *Winchester '73* [1950]) as former gunslinger and now town drunk Al Denton, who briefly regains his speed and accuracy with a gun that materializes out of thin air seemingly because of a pointed glance by Henry J. Fate (Malcolm Atterbury), a traveling peddler passing through town. With the gun, Denton is able to defeat the bully Hotaling (Martin Landau) with some remarkable shooting. However, as a result, Denton gains a reputation, and immediately another young hotshot, Pete Grant (Doug McClure), rides into town to challenge him. The desperate Denton relies on a magic potion from Fate that will give him deadly accuracy for ten seconds. But when the young gunfighter enters the saloon for the showdown and Denton gulps the contents of his vial—he sees his opponent doing the same thing! The two men shoot the guns out of each other's hands at the same time, both being injured so that, according to the town doctor's immediate prognosis, neither will ever be able to handle a gun again. The episode concludes with Denton philosophizing that they both have received a blessing in disguise because they are now relieved of the burden of having constantly to kill in defense of their reputations.

While the episode is one of the few in which fate works benignly and the protagonists end up better off, it does make use of familiar elements of the Western—the settings, the costumes, the code of the gunfight—but mixes in a fantastical aspect, well before the development of the hybrid genre of "the weird Western." Most obviously, it makes use of the Western's most basic visual opposition: Denton wears a white cowboy hat, while both Hotaling and Grant wear black hats and are dressed in black. The Western genre also provides the stock characters that populate the episode's town: the bartender, the sympathetic saloon girl, the impetuous young gun. In one of the earliest academic studies of the Western as a genre, published during the show's run in 1961, Peter Homans described the typical town of Westerns at the time as consisting of "Jerry-built, slapped-together buildings, with false fronts lined awkwardly along a road that is forever thick with dust or mud" (135)—exactly like the unnamed town in the episode. Further, of the town's few buildings, the saloon is the most important because "it is the only place in the entire story where people can be seen together time after time. It thereby performs the function of a meeting-house, social center, church, and so on" and is also the space where the climax plays out (136)—again, exactly the case in "Mr. Denton on Doomsday." (The same convention is played upon in a different way in the later "Mr. Garrity and the Graves.") Even the men in the bar and the henchmen of the two young guns are exactly as Homans describes them: "The boys," as he calls them, "those drinking, bearded, grimy people who are always 'just there,' drinking and gambling in the saloon, without any apparent interest in anyone or anything," necessary only as an audience for the confrontation (138).

Some of the scenes in the episode are standard in Western films. Denton's amazing gunplay, his shot through the chain holding the chandelier and sending it down, knocking the gun from Hotaling's hand, is like the trick shooting on display by the heroes of so many Westerns (compare, for example, the gunplay performed by Dean Martin's Dude in *Rio Bravo* [1959], also in a saloon among the boys, released in the same year as "Denton" was broadcast). The scene where Denton practices shooting with cans on a fence similarly recalls any number of Westerns when, say, the Easterner learns to handle a gun, as in John Ford's *The Man Who Shot Liberty Valance* (1964). When Denton regains his self-respect, he goes to the barber for a shave, the "civilizing" sense of the scene recalling Wyatt Earp's tonsorial visit in Ford's *My Darling Clementine* (1946)—but in this case Fate's visage is reflected in the barber's window, underscoring the show's fantastic aspect. Denton's potential future

"The boys" witness the shootout in "Mr. Denton on Doomsday."

of forever facing challenges from impetuous youths is exactly the dilemma that confronts such protagonists of "adult Westerns" as Johnny Ringo (Gregory Peck) in *The Gunfighter* (1950). While Ringo deliberately passes on his reputation as a burden to the youngster who shoots him in the back as revenge, in "Doomsday" Denton—and his adversary—are redeemed (the saloon as "church") because they can no longer shoot. This is a rare upbeat ending for the show, a more pacifistic message and a stark reversal of the tragic dimension of the adult psychological Western as represented by *The Gunfighter*, but one consistent with Serling's hope for peace among men.

As the presence of Duryea in the episode also suggests, the show also frequently relied on the iconography and mise-en-scène of film noir (Duryea also appeared in several noirs including Fritz Lang's *The Woman in the Window* [1944] and *Scarlet*

Street [1945]). Hollywood veteran George T. Clemens shot the majority of *Twilight Zone* episodes (117 of 156), but no matter who was behind the camera, when a character on the show succumbed to emotional duress—as they often did—there promptly would appear images of blinking neon with canted angles, streets wet with pools of water and light, all evoking, as in noir, a fallen world of corruption and evil or the madness of the protagonist. Such imagery is prominent right from the pilot episode, "Where Is Everybody?" (1.1: October 2, 1959): in the opening stinger before Serling's introduction, every shot features a canted angle, sometimes the camera even tilting as it moves.

The episode "Execution" mentioned earlier makes use of both film noir and the Western with a science-fiction premise in its story of a cowboy outlaw, Joe Caswell, who is plucked from the Wild West of the past and teleported through time to a modern city where he becomes, as the scientist responsible puts it, "a nineteenth-century primitive in a twentieth-century jungle." In the opening scene the murderous Caswell is about to be hanged by a lynch mob in what the sheriff describes as a civic service, but Caswell mocks his executioners' belief in justice. The set, with its clearly painted backdrop of a sky against which hangs the noose, recalls the eerie artificiality of *The Ox-Bow Incident* (1943), which, like this episode, raises questions about justice and retribution within the context of lynching and vigilantism (a theme that Serling already had explored in his earlier teleplays, as discussed previously). Once he disappears from the noose and reappears in the scientist's lab, the story seems to switch from Western to science fiction, but then, when Caswell kills Manion and goes out into the city night, the world becomes, from his perspective, a noirish jumble of urban horror. Even before, as soon as Caswell states his desire to see "that world out there," suddenly the mise-en-scène shifts to the excess expressionism characteristic of film noir as lights begin to flash on and off outside through the window curtains. When

Caswell goes outside, the shots shift to canted and dramatic low angles, and the pace of the editing, which had been relatively leisurely to this point, picks up considerably—techniques inherited from classic Hollywood cinema that the show employed frequently at such moments. Glaring lights from a generic "The Joint" and the ironically named "Jim Henry's Paradise," along with the inevitable jukebox blaring some pseudomodernist jazz, intrude on Caswell, who describes this "urban jungle"—the space of noir—as "carriages without horses, and those lights going on and off all the time, and the noise."

The hall of mirrors in "What You Need" (1.12: December 25, 1959) specifically evokes the climax of Orson Welles's classic noir *The Lady from Shanghai* (1947), while "In Praise of Pip" (5.1: September 27, 1963) features a supernatural meeting between a father and his dying son in a timeless carnival of the imagination, the images evocative of and undoubtedly influenced by such noirs as *Nightmare Alley* (1947) and *Gun Crazy* (1950), which also feature scenes in carnivals.* In their book on *The Twilight Zone* Don Presnell and Marty McGee rightly describe the episode "Nervous Man in a Four Dollar Room"

* The show also made striking expressionist use of sound. Clearly, the production crew were aware of the expressive possibilities of the soundtrack: the muffled sound of the human voices in the enormous model showroom—a touch worthy of Orson Welles—beautifully expresses the overwhelming emotions of Mr. and Mrs. Holt as they try to absorb the possibilities of the services offered by the New Life Corporation in "The Trade-Ins." "The Fever," for example, features the manipulated recorded sound of clinking coins to give chilling voice to a slot machine; "The Mighty Casey" adds comic sound effects to accentuate its sight gags; and "Sounds and Silences" offers an extended use of subjective sound to convey the growing madness of the protagonist (John McGiver). "King Nine Will Not Return" and "The Hitch-Hiker" rely on close-ups combined with subjective voice-overs rather than conventional dialogue. And in "The Invaders" Agnes Moorehead has no dialogue at all, the fear and tension in the episode driven instead by periods of silence punctuated only by her groans and cries.

(2.3: October 14, 1960) as "really a half-hour film noir" (72). "Perchance to Dream" (1.9: November 27, 1959), directed by Robert Florey, responsible for numerous atmospheric B-films, also mobilizes many elements of noir, here stylized to obvious excess because the images are framed as part of one character's Freudian nightmare. The presence of Richard Conte (featured in such notable noirs as *Call Northside 777* [1948], *The Blue Gardenia* [1953], and *The Big Combo* [1955]) as besieged protagonist Edward Hall helps establish the noir atmosphere, and the undulating Suzanne Lloyd as Maya, the femme fatale luring him to his doom, is wholly archetypal, lacking any actual characterization.

A number of the show's writers and directors had experience making film noir. Robert Florey, a Hollywood stalwart whose credits include the horror thrillers *Murders in the Rue Morgue* (1932) and *The Beast with Five Fingers* (1946), directed three episodes of

Maya (Suzanne Lloyd) as the archetypal femme fatale in "Perchance to Dream."

The Twilight Zone, as did Mitchell Leisen, who had made many melodramas for Paramount, including the fantasy *Death Takes a Holiday* (1934). Martin M. Goldsmith, writer of the episodes "The Encounter" (5.31: May 1, 1964) and "What's in the Box" (5.24: March 13, 1964), also wrote several noirs, including the screenplay of *Detour* (1945) and story for *The Narrow Margin* (1952). Jacques Tourneur, responsible for classics of both noir (*Out of the Past* [1947]) and atmospheric horror (*Cat People* [1942], *I Walked with a Zombie* [1943]), appropriately directed the moody episode "Night Call" (5.19: February 7, 1964), about a woman who is terrified by a voice on her telephone that turns out to be her dead husband's. Don Siegel, responsible for two episodes ("Uncle Simon" [5.8: November 15, 1963] and "The Self-Improvement of Salvadore Ross" [5.17: January 17, 1964]), had directed *The Big Steal* (1949), *Riot in Cell Block 11* (1954), *Private Hell 36* (1954), and the noir-infused horror classic, *Invasion of the Body Snatchers* (1956). And John Brahm, who directed twelve episodes (among them, "Time Enough at Last")—more than any other director—had made the fine noirs *The Lodger* (1944), *Hangover Square* (1945), and *The Locket* (1946) as well as *The Undying Monster* (1942), a generic blend of mystery and horror.

Serling himself clearly admired genre fiction and often sought to emulate the punchy style of the pulps. His prologue for "Mr. Dingle, the Strong" (2.19: March 3, 1961), for example, could be mistaken for the tough prose of Dashiell Hammett or Raymond Chandler, hard-boiled writers whose work was a major influence on the development of film noir:

> Uniquely American institution known as the neighborhood bar. Reading left to right are Mr. Anthony O'Toole, proprietor, who waters his drinks like geraniums but who stands foursquare for peace and quiet and for booths for ladies. This is Mr. Joseph J. Callahan, an unregistered bookie, whose entire life is any sporting event with two sides and a set of odds. His idea of a meeting at the summit is any dialogue

> between a catcher and a pitcher with more than one man on base. And this animated citizen is every anonymous bettor who ever dropped rent money on a race horse, a prize fight, or a floating crap game, and who took out his frustrations and his insolvency on any vulnerable fellow barstool companion within arm's and fist's reach. And this is Mr. Luther Dingle, a vacuum-cleaner salesman whose volume of business is roughly that of a valet at a hobo convention.

But then Serling drops in the science-fiction line: "And these two unseen gentlemen are visitors from outer space."

As Booker observes, the show's evocation of film noir was "no doubt largely because the hundreds of films noir made during the 1940s and 1950s had already demonstrated that dim lighting and exaggerated shadow effects could produce precisely the air of mystery and foreboding that *The Twilight Zone* was striving for" (55). (It does not matter that "film noir" was not an operative generic term in the United States at the time but was applied retrospectively later on; the gangster and detective films, mysteries, thrillers, and crime movies that comprise noir were still regarded in generic terms.) But, as well, by evoking traditional genres the show could connect simultaneously to adult viewers already trained in the traditions of classic Hollywood and to a younger demographic growing up in the atomic era that was more appreciative of science fiction and horror, which, like film noir, also relied heavily on expressionist techniques.

Variety's contemporary review of the show said it was "generic in its appeal" yet avoided "the current westerns and private eyes" (Grams, 66), failing to note how it nevertheless used elements of them. Stephen King is more appreciative of the show's unusual generic hybridity: "It was not a western or a cop show (although some of the stories had western formats or featured cops 'n' robbers); it was not really a science-fiction show (although *The Complete Directory to Prime Time Network*

TV Shows categorizes it as such); not a sitcom (although some of the episodes were funny); not really occult (although it did occult stories frequently—in its own peculiar fashion), not really supernatural. It was its own thing." (King, 229). The atmospheric "Jess-Belle" (4.7: February 14, 1963), written by Earl Hamner Jr., serves as a good example. Set in the Blue Ridge Mountains, the atmospheric story tells of an engaged couple, Billy-Ben Turner (James Best) and Elly Glover (Laura Devon), and the jealous former girlfriend Jess-Belle (Anne Francis) who wants Billy-Ben for her own. She drinks a magic potion given to her by the witch Granny Hart (Jeannette Nolan) in order to get him, which she does but with unintended consequences. Presnell and McGee rightly describe the moody episode as "a smorgasbord of literary and film genres: folktale, ghost story, love story, and Southern Gothic" (145).

For film scholar Rick Worland, regardless of the generic trappings of a given episode, *The Twilight Zone* was "generally intended to frighten" (Worland, 104). In their book on the show, Presnell and McGee provide an appendix that groups episodes according to "genres, themes, and plot devices," with the grouping for "fear and paranoia" being three times as long as any other (242–52). A few episodes such as "The Hitch-Hiker" (1.16: January 22, 1960), "The Grave" (3.7: October 27, 1961), and "Spur of the Moment" (5.21: February 21, 1964) are clearly exercises in horror, employing, like many other episodes, familiar horror tropes—darkness and shadows, eerie stretches of silence, a sense of helplessness and fear of the unknown—along with a heavily expressionist look to provide a sense of terror and suspense. These horror elements dominate several episodes, including "The Howling Man" (2.5: November 4, 1960), a Gothic chiller written by Charles Beaumont and directed by stalwart television director Douglas Heyes, also responsible for eight other episodes including "The After Hours" and "Eye of the Beholder." The Gothic has rarely appeared in network television series, and when it has, it has tended to be treated as camp (*Dark Shadows* [ABC, 1966–71]) or comedy (*The Addams Family* [ABC, 1964–66]), but not on *The Twilight Zone*.

"The Howling Man" begins with a shot of a violent thunderstorm and flashing lightning as the camera tracks back to reveal a man (H. M. Wynant) who, with clear urgency and distress, talks directly to the camera—in a canted-angle shot, already—exhorting us to believe, because "we must," the bizarre story he is about to tell. A dissolve introduces a flashback that brings us to another storm, sometime after World War I, when the man, whose name is Ellington, loses his way during a walking trip in central Europe. Feverish and in need of shelter, he comes upon an old mansion that looms up forebodingly in the darkness like Manderley in *Rebecca* (1940). The camera tilts to one side or the other as it tracks to follow Ellington, matching his feverishness. In the mansion Ellington discovers what seems to be a group of mad monks led by Brother Jerome (John Carradine) who have imprisoned a man in a cell. The mise-en-scène of the mansion is replete with signifiers of Gothic menace, and the casting of Carradine as Jerome lends the episode the patina of a B-movie thriller, making us wonder whether Jerome is insane.

The man in the cell (Robin Hughes) claims to be an innocent victim of a self-righteous sect and begs to be released. Ellington demands an explanation of Brother Jerome, who reluctantly reveals that it is no man they have captured but the Devil himself, contained in his cell through the power of a wooden pole he calls "the staff of Truth" that bars the door and can only be removed by a human. Ellington pretends to believe Jerome, but when alone he takes the opportunity to remove the staff from the door and release the prisoner, who promptly transforms into the Devil, complete with goatee, cape, and proverbial horns. Shortly thereafter, World War II erupts. As the flashback ends, we learn that Ellington, realizing what he has done, has devoted his life to recapturing the Devil, a goal that he has now at long last succeeded in achieving. His story is

The feverish Ellington (H. M. Wynant) in "The Howling Man," an exercise in Gothic horror.

being told to his housekeeper as Ellington is about to leaves his quarters to arrange for the transportation of his prisoner back to the hermitage. But despite his explicit instructions to her, she lifts the piece of wood straddling the door, which swings open ominously . . .

"The Invaders" (2.15: January 27, 1961) is similarly infused with an atmosphere of Gothic horror, here enhanced by the absence of dialogue (although there are occasional cries, whimpers, and grunts) until very near the end. An unnamed woman (Agnes Moorehead) living in a remote country shack "untouched by human progress," as Serling vaguely tells us in his introduction, hears a strange sound coming from above. Going to investigate, she discovers a tiny flying saucer in the rafters, out of which two little humanoid figures in protective suits emerge. For virtually the entire episode, the woman plays a cat-and-mouse game with the two creatures, who pop up in various places around the cabin as she tries to kill them with whatever she has at hand. In the end, when the woman returns to the attic and smashes the saucer with an axe, we glimpse a "US Air Force: Space Probe 1" logo on it and hear the voice of one of the little "creatures" calling "Central Control" on the ship's radio and shouting a warning to stay away from this planet with its race of overpowering giants. In addition to its Gothic atmosphere, the production design of the episode may seem sparse, but it brilliantly presents a rough pioneer look, a perception encouraged by Serling's opening comments, that at the same time appears sufficiently indistinct so as not to suggest a specific period of American history, thus making the twist more effectively surprising.

Of course, other episodes employed other modes of the fantastic and were quite different in tone. "The Fugitive" (3.25: March 9, 1962) serves as a good example. In the story, old Ben (J. Pat O'Malley) befriends his neighbor Jenny (Susan Gordon), a young girl with a leg brace. Ben confides to Jenny that he is an alien fleeing from two men (also aliens) who want to return him to his home world against his will. John Sayles later used a similar premise in *The Brother from Another Planet* (1984), giving it a racial theme, but Charles Beaumont's script here is much more upbeat: as it turns out, Ben is not an escaped prisoner or slave but a revered king whom the people want to return. Ben finally agrees and contrives a way to take Jenny with him. Serling then comes on to explain that Ben actually looks like a handsome young man, and that although her humorless aunt (Nancy Kulp) will find her missing, Jenny "will grow up to be an honest-to-goodness queen—somewhere in the Twilight Zone." The episode thus combines the science-fiction premise of a shape-shifting alien with the Cinderella fairy tale of a little girl who lives happily ever after with her Prince Charming.

Fairy tales are also invoked by the title of the episode "Once upon a Time" (3.13: December 15, 1961), a whimsical vehicle for Buster Keaton, and by the opening of "The Mighty Casey" (1.35: June 17, 1960), in which Serling uses the phrase twice, the second time saying that "since this is strictly a story of make-believe, it has to start this way: Once upon a time, in Hoboken, New Jersey . . ." Fantasy narratives are based neither in the natural world of science fiction nor in the supernatural world of horror but in an alternate reality. As science-fiction writer Robert Heinlein has noted, "Science fiction and fantasy are as different as Karl Marx and Groucho Marx. Fantasy is constructed either by denying the real world in toto or at least by making a prime basis of the story one or more admittedly false premises—fairies, talking mules, trips through a looking glass, vampires, seacoast Bohemia, Mickey Mouse" (Heinlein, 8). As different as these genres are for some critics, however, *The Twilight Zone* employed them all, mixing them like little Anthony Freemont's hybridized creatures in "It's a Good Life." "Once Upon a Time," for example, places a science-fiction robot in a whimsical sports fantasy.

Serling himself sometimes addressed the distinctions between the fantastic genres in his remarks to the audience. He begins his opening monologue for "The Fugitive" by discussing the difference between science fiction and fantasy, describing the former as making the probable possible and the latter as rendering the impossible probable, and then suggesting that tonight's tale shows what happens when you put those two things together. He introduces the episode "The Obsolete Man" (2.29: June 2, 1961), set in an Orwellian future, by remarking that the tale isn't a story of "a future that will be, but what might be"—in other words, it is fictional extrapolation rather than scientific prognostication. As Serling goes on to observe, "This is not a new world but simply an extension of what began in the old one," an explicit statement about the workings of science fiction set in the future, whether utopian or dystopian. Similarly, he concludes the story of "The Old Man in the Cave" (5.7: November 8, 1963), about a group of atomic war survivors whose society is regulated by an unseen computer, by observing that the episode is "not a prediction of what is to be, just a projection of what could be."

In "Will the Real Martian Please Stand Up?," about a group of travelers stranded in a diner during a snowstorm, one of whom might be an alien, character actor Jack Elam delightedly exclaims, "She's just like a science fiction, that's what she is! A regular Ray Bradbury!" (According to Zicree, Bradbury, along with Heinlein and Isaac Asimov, were Serling's favorite science-fiction writers, and references to Bradbury appear in at least two other episodes—the name of the character Dr. Bradbury in "Walking Distance" and the "Bradbury account" in "A Stop at Willoughby" [Zicree 273].) But ultimately *The Twilight Zone*, because of its generic hybridity, might best be categorized more broadly as speculative fiction. Narrative theorist Robert Scholes argues that, rather than striving for a mimetic rendering of the world as realist fiction does, speculative narrative instead "offers us a world clearly and radically discontinuous from the one we know yet returns to confront that known world in some cognitive way" (Scholes, 29). Although Scholes's focus was science-fiction literature, this is a perfect description of the viewing experience in the case of *The Twilight Zone*, for each episode aimed to do precisely that. The show's distinctive twist endings, discussed further in chapter 4, function to this end, making us rethink all we had seen previously in the episode and consequently our moral, social, and philosophical assumptions. Carl Plantinga refers to these endings as "frame shifters," endings that challenge "conformist frames of reference" (54).

Other critics have made similar arguments to Scholes's regarding the potentially subversive and liberating qualities of the different forms of speculative narrative. In her influential analysis of fantasy texts, for example, Rosemary Jackson argues that all fantasy narratives necessarily express some form of desire, for wanting something that is lacking. Thus, as Jackson writes, fantasy's "excursion into disorder can only begin from

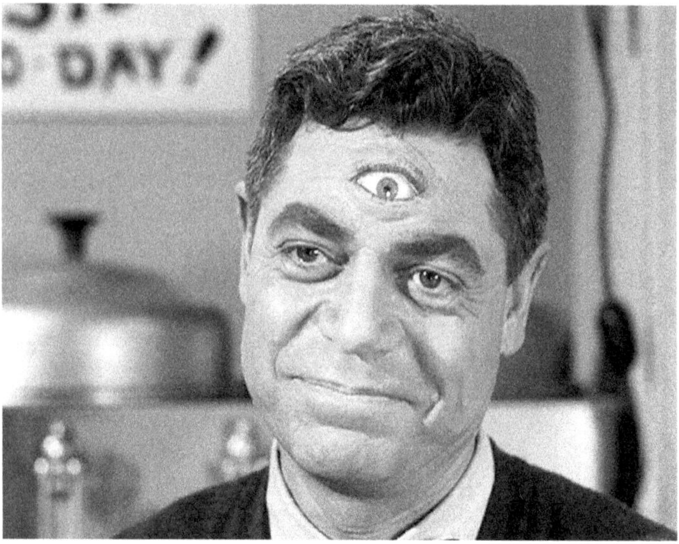

Barney Phillips as the Venusian revealed in "Will the Real Martian Please Stand Up?"

a base within the dominant cultural order," so that fantasy always has the potential to be "a telling index of the limits of that order. Its introduction of the 'unreal' is set against the category of the 'real'—a category which the fantastic interrogates by its difference" (4). Jackson's claim that any given work of fantasy will either "tell of, manifest, or show desire" or "expel" desire when it disturbs the "dominant social order" (4) is similar to Robin Wood's pioneering theorization of the radical or subversive potential in horror. Wood sees horror as articulating the Freudian notion of the return of the repressed, those wishes and desires we secretly harbor but guiltily try to deny. For him, the fundamental subject of horror is "the struggle for recognition of all that our civilization *re*presses or *op*presses." In every horror text this "monstrousness" is set against normality, again providing the possibility of examining the monster or expelling it (9–11). Conservative or, in Wood's terms, "reactionary" horror films tend toward the latter, seeing the monster merely as other and a threat to be destroyed, while "progressive" horror movies position the monster more sympathetically, as the result of a repressive society. Many *Twilight Zone* episodes are easily read as psychological horror tales with the fantastic element explicable as the outward projection of the protagonist's guilt, desire, or fear: "Perchance to Dream," "The Fever" (1.17: January 29, 1960), "Nightmare as a Child," "A Stop at Willoughby," "Static," "The Mirror" (3.6: October 20, 1961), and "Sounds and Silences" (5.27: April 3, 1964) just a few among them. Exactly how subversive *The Twilight Zone* in fact was is discussed later, but certainly the intent of the show was to critique multiple aspects of contemporary society.

Serling's explicit invocation of the "dimension of imagination" is of a piece with that philosophical openness described as "a sense of wonder" that some early critics of science fiction, writing contemporaneously with Serling, saw as fundamental to the genre. Damon Knight famously regarded this sense of wonder as "some widening of the mind's horizons, no matter in what direction," and said it "is what science fiction is all about" (13). Sam Moskowitz, writing slightly later, similarly defined it as a heightened awareness and open attitude to new ideas or alternative possibilities (211). In the world of *The Twilight Zone*, those who have "more temper than imagination," like Jenny's dour aunt in "The Fugitive," or who refuse to think young and "kick the can," are forever constrained by the here and now. It is precisely because boxer Bolie Jackson (Ivan Dixon) is unable to accept the possibility of magic in "The Big Tall Wish" that he finds himself remaining the loser rather than the winner of his big bout.

Although the show's famous opening changed several times during its initial run, common to each version, like variations of a theme, is the idea that the place called "the Twilight Zone" is that potentially unbounded space limited only by the "imagination."

Significantly, it is when Serling says this word in the first-season opening that the camera seems to tilt up to reveal the sky and the familiar twinkling stars of the show's graphic logo, as if the image were opening outward to embrace the limitless possibilities of the universe—in other words, the sense of wonder. In the last version of the opening, a number of objects traverse the screen relating to Serling's monologue, including an opening door (Aldous Huxley's "doors of perception") and a rotating spiral that could be seen by the viewer as swirling in or out, depending on one's perception ("imagination"). It may be that the show's various openings reveal "a motif of transition, of the movement between positions" that "prepares the viewer for the sudden switches and juxtapositions the show uses to make its points" (Mortenson, 61), but perhaps more importantly, such an open frame of mind called for in the opening was regarded as essential for appreciating stories of the fantastic.

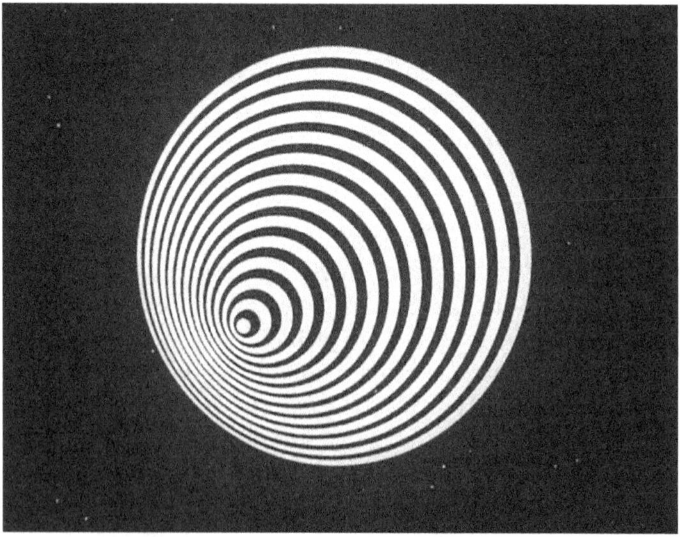

The animated spiral in the fifth-season opening.

Whether individual episodes mobilized elements of fantasy, science fiction, or horror, *The Twilight Zone*'s approach was decidedly more "soft" than "hard," that is, less concerned with the science and technology of its premises than with their cultural and psychological implications. In "On Thursday We Leave for Home" (4.16: May 2, 1963), about the rescue of a desperate group of colonists on a parched planet after thirty years, the commander of the rescue ship (Tim O'Connor) tells "Captain" William Benteen (James Whitmore), who has been responsible for maintaining the group's morale all those years, that his community is a false one because it's like a "test tube"—"antiseptic and germ free. And also sterile," isolated from the actual complexities of the world—not unlike the way the show itself used various generic contexts to contain its moral fables. As mentioned, the fantastic element of many of the episodes can be "explained" as psychological trauma—"Nightmare as a Child," in which the strange little girl that Helen Foley meets turns out to be herself as a child and who helps her to remember the repressed memories of her mother's murder, serves as a perfect model. But how, for example, does a scientist invent a time machine? How does a camera come to record the future? Where does the extraordinary timepiece in "A Kind of Stopwatch" (5.4: October 18, 1963) come from? Such questions frequently go unanswered on the show, and for many purists this is the reason why *The Twilight Zone* cannot be considered science fiction. Witchcraft, magic, necromancy, alchemy, and the simply unexplained provide the premise for *Twilight Zone* episodes as often as aliens and technology. "Death is relative and there may not be an end"—that is all the explanation for his resurrection the ghost of Shakespeare provides in "The Bard" (4.18: May 23, 1963).

Science Fiction Theatre (syndication, 1955–57) began each episode with the camera panning slowly across the various pieces of high-tech equipment in a lab, emphasizing that show's technological emphasis from the outset, even before host

Truman Bradley appeared to welcome viewers and offer an illustrative experiment. By contrast, Serling's introductory narrations more often than not focused on people rather than props: "You're about to meet a hypochondriac. Witness Mr. Walter Bedeker . . ." ("Escape Clause" [1.6: November 6, 1959]); "Portrait of a bush-league fuehrer named Peter Vollmer, a sparse little man who feeds off his self-delusions and finds himself perpetually hungry for want of greatness in his diet" ("He's Alive" [4.4: January 24, 1963]); "Portrait of a man at work . . ." ("A Nice Place to Visit"); "Portrait of a nervous man . . ." ("You Drive" [5.14: January 3, 1964]); and so on. Tellingly, when Serling adapted the science-fiction story "What You Need" by "Lewis Padgett" (pseudonym of Henry Kuttner and C. L. Moore) for the show, he eliminated the premise of a scientist who invents a machine that allows him to see the future of other people and instead bestows the inexplicable ability of prognostication upon his protagonist, a kindly street peddler (Ernest Truex) who gives people apparently mundane things that eventually prove important. For Serling, the focus is always on the man, not the machine. Even while working on *The Twilight Zone*, Serling was selling another series concept, this one for a Western (dominating the airwaves at the time with shows such as *Gunsmoke*, *Wagon Train* [NBC, 1957–65], *Bonanza*, *Have Gun—Will Travel* [CBS, 1957–63], and *Wanted Dead or Alive* [CBS, 1958–61], some of them among the most popular shows ever) called *The Loner* [CBS, 1965–66] that would focus on character rather than action. (Starring Lloyd Bridges, it failed to survive one full season.)

The show's minimal reliance on special effects follows from its soft approach to the fantastic. In the visual media speculative stories have relied heavily on special effects since George Méliès's *A Trip to the Moon* (1902), a reliance that has become even more intense since the development of the science-fiction blockbuster with *Star Wars* in 1977 and *Superman* in 1978 and then computer-generated imagery (CGI) in films such as

Jurassic Park (1993). Indeed, these effects in turn constitute one of the special pleasures of the genre. They show us exciting things that are in fact impossible or at least as yet unrealized in the real world; we marvel at special-effects images at once for their fantastic content and for the power of their realization, paradoxically enjoying them precisely because we know they are unreal, but we suspend our disbelief anyway and allow ourselves to be convinced of them. ("You'll believe a man can fly" promised the promotional copy for the 1978 *Superman*). And so for many viewers, nothing destroys the pleasure of a science-fiction movie more than seeing the seams in a matte shot or glimpsing the zipper on a monster's bodysuit.

Jason Mittell argues that recent "complex" television series encourage an "operational aesthetic" in viewers whereby they "simultaneously care about the story and marvel at its telling" (2015, 46), offering special effects ("moments of spectacle") as especially intense instances of the operational aesthetic at work. But, as Lester H. Hunt notes, while fantasy and science fiction are associated with visual effects, "It is really remarkable how many of the episodes [of *The Twilight Zone*] consist mainly of two or three characters talking to each other" (7). Although the average budget per episode was approximately $55,000 (the pilot cost an impressive $75,000), which was slightly higher than that of other programs that debuted on CBS that season such as *The Many Loves of Dobie Gillis* (1959–63: $40,000), *Johnny Ringo* (1959–60: $45,000), and *The Betty Hutton Show* (1959: $50,000) (Grams, 64; see also Presnell and McGee, 14), extensive special effects were still largely prohibitive for a television series and were often avoided. The episode "The Odyssey of Flight 33" (2.18: February 24, 1961), about a commercial airliner that travels back in time when it is caught in a strange jet stream, features a shot of a stop-motion dinosaur animation that, at $2,500, was the most expensive special effect ever used in the show (Presnell and McGee, 87).

Because cost has always been a significant issue for science-fiction and fantasy television series, especially before the use of

CGI, *The Twilight Zone* featured surprisingly few special effects. In "The Fear" (5.35: May 29, 1964), something of a reversal of "The Invaders," there is a matte shot of a giant one-eyed alien towering over the landscape. This shot offers a particularly interesting twist, as at first it looks like a poorly done special effect, but eventually the narrative reveals that this is precisely what it is, for it turns out to be a not very convincing giant balloon belonging to diminutive aliens who, much smaller than humans, are afraid of being overpowered and crushed by the Terran giants and so in effect have used cheap special effects to create the illusion of being large to scare people off. We might read this as a reflexive joke about the show's limitations regarding special effects, just as the aliens in "Mr. Dingle, the Strong"—a Martian with two heads in a single suit and two short and shuffling Venusians with moustaches—might be understood as "poking fun at low-budget sci-fi from the period" rather than just "silly" (Presnell and McGee, 88).

To create the effect of the nuclear blast in "Time Enough at Last," the bank vault set in which Bemis is sitting when it detonates was built on springs, allowing the set and the camera to shake together (Zicree, 69). But such relatively elaborate mechanical special-effects shots were rare for *The Twilight Zone*. Many of the show's special effects tended to be ingeniously simple and low tech, like an empty mirror frame allowing the face of Arch Hammer to seem to change to that of Foster (Ross Martin) in one shot as the camera pans from Hammer shaving to the "mirror" in "The Four of Us Are Dying" (Zicree, 87). The tiny human "aliens" of "The Invaders" were merely little puppets animated by the director's fingers inserted into their backs (Zicree, 172–75). In "Black Leather Jackets" (5.18: January 31, 1964) the aliens just wear said article of clothing and ride motorcycles, sort of extraterrestrial Wild Ones that also recall the very low-budget aliens who wear sunglasses and business suits in Roger Corman's *Not of this Earth* (1957). Relatively simple optical effects like freeze-frame photography are central to the episode "A Kind of a Stopwatch," in which a man (Richard Erdmann) discovers a timepiece that has the power to stop the world in its tracks. (Earlier, in the episode "Elegy," where three astronauts land on a remote asteroid and discover familiar tableaux of small-town Americana, the actors simply stood still in position, a strategy, alas, periodically noticeable.) The switch of Bolie Jackson and his opponent Joey Consiglio in the ring in "The Big Tall Wish" is also achieved simply by a series of freeze frames.

The Twilight Zone also saved money by recycling existing footage. The final shot of aliens departing Earth in "The Monsters Are Due on Maple Street" was actually taken from MGM's science-fiction film *Forbidden Planet* (1956) and run upside down and backward (Zicree, 92). Props from that classic science-fiction movie pop up periodically in the show, from the model spaceship in "The Invaders" to the interiors of the spaceship cabins in

The aliens of "Mr. Dingle, the Strong."

"People Are Alike All Over," "Third from the Sun," "Elegy," and "Death Ship" (4.6: February 7, 1963) to the appearance of Robby the Robot in "Uncle Simon" and "The Brain Center at Whipple's" (5.33: May 15, 1964). A diminutive Robby also makes an appearance in the first shot of "One for the Angels": when the camera pans down from the opening twilight sky, the first thing we see is a windup toy Robby, one of the items being sold by pitchman Lew Bookman (Ed Wynn). Production space for *The Twilight Zone* was rented at MGM, allowing the show's makers access to the studio's back lot and sets as well as props from other films in addition to *Forbidden Planet*. Sets from *The Wreck of the Mary Deare* (1959), for example, were used for the filming of the episode "Judgment Night" (1.10: December 4, 1959), and houses built for the Smith family's street in *Meet Me in St. Louis* (1944) were used in the nostalgic "Walking Distance" (Presnell and McGee, 42).

Each week *The Twilight Zone* offered a different take on established genres, the show displaying no uniform generic consistency from episode to episode. The same might be said of any given episode's affective tone. One episode might be a grimly ironic cautionary tale about nuclear holocaust, like "Time Enough at Last" or "The Shelter"; another a slapstick comedy or a thriller about time travel like "Once upon a Time" and "Back There" (2.13: January 13, 1961) respectively; and yet another a sentimental, Runyonesque fantasy like "Night of the Meek" (2.11: December 23, 1960), with Art Carney as a drunken department-store Santa who finds the real Santa's toy sack and consequently a purpose in life. While genre has always been crucial to television, and television shows routinely mix genres (Mittell 2004: xii–xiii), *The Twilight Zone* was the only weekly series that blended genres differently from episode to episode rather than simply as a hybridized premise for a continuing narrative. Viewers never knew what generic stew a new episode would offer and consequently, what emotions it might elicit—suspense, humor, fear, or wonder. This unpredictability was an essential part of the show's appeal even as it left viewers uncertain about what was to come in a given episode. Thus, the "operational aesthetic" was at work in *The Twilight Zone* not just with the ending of episodes and their frequent narrative twists and the summary observations by Serling but even before an episode began as viewers wondered what *kind* of story they were going to be seeing.

In 1961 broadcasting historian Eric Barnouw bemoaned the generic nature of television, specifically referring to Rod Serling and *The Twilight Zone*. After praising the writers of "Golden Age" television drama, he said that "The author of *Requiem for a Heavyweight* now writes formula mysteries of the supernatural and even wins prizes for them: a symptom of the low estate to which television drama has fallen, in just a few short years" (qtd. in Boddy 1990, 193). However, it is important to remember that auteurs—those artists who work within collaborative mass media but nevertheless maintain a personal vision—of necessity make use of generic material. As Lawrence Alloway noted regarding cinema, "The personal contribution of many directors can only be seen fully after typical iconographic elements have been identified" (41). Genre, in other words, provides the background against which the author's personal vision may be seen—a point no less true for television than it is for cinema. How Rod Serling, television's "first auteur" (Brode and Serling, 233–34), used genres in *The Twilight Zone*, is explored further in the following chapter.

2

"The Prime Mover"

The Twilight Zone and Authorship

Like many of the television anthology dramas that preceded it, *The Twilight Zone* featured a host to "frame" episodes, introducing them to viewers and then returning at the end to wrap them up with some final comments. This was common practice for anthology drama series, as with, for example, *Dick Powell's Zane Gray Theater* (CBS, 1956–61) and *The David Niven Show* (1959). Sometimes, as with *The Barbara Stanwyck Show* (NBC, 1960–61) and *The Loretta Young Show* (NBC, 1953–61), the star host also acted in some of the episodes. Whether they did or not, though, most of these hosts were movie stars who brought a familiar persona to the small screen, helping, like *The Twilight Zone*'s use of genre, to transition a generation of moviegoers to the relatively new medium of television as well as providing a sense of continuity from week to week.

Other similarly themed television shows to *The Twilight Zone* that also featured a host include the aforementioned *Science Fiction Theatre*, hosted by Truman Bradley, and the concurrent *Alcoa Presents: One Step Beyond* (ABC, 1959–61), hosted by John Newland. Treading in the occasionally overlapping genres of thriller, suspense, mystery, and the macabre, *Alfred Hitchcock Presents* (CBS, 1955–60, 1962–64; NBC, 1960–62, 1964–65) brought household recognition to the director and his trademark droll sense of humor. Literally stepping into his caricatured profile at the beginning of each episode, Hitchcock on the weekly show that bore his name—despite his relative lack of involvement in the show's production—was a vivid demonstration of the power of television's recent but already primary place in the dynamics of celebrity culture, a benefit that Serling, too, would reap once he began to appear before the camera with his prologues beginning with the second-season opener, "King Nine Will Not Return" (2.1: September 30, 1960). Both Truman Bradley and John Newland were actors with a few small and unmemorable performances to their credit who became better known for their television hosting roles, yet even more than they, Serling became recognizable everywhere as the host of *The Twilight Zone*, a role he hadn't initially planned on assuming but for which he was perfect. Zicree claims that "Rod Serling had become the most famous writer in America, if not the world" by the time the series finished its initial five-year run (204).

Several earlier horror and fantasy radio shows from the 1930s through the 1950s relied on the use of a host to provide an established format, beginning with Old Nancy and her cat Satan on *The Witch's Tale* (1931–38) and including related shows such as *Inner Sanctum Mystery* (1941–52) and *The Whistler* (1941–55). Serling learned much from these and other radio shows written by Wyllis Cooper and Arch Oboler, such as *Lights Out*, first on radio (1934–47) and then television (NBC, 1949–52). (Serling liked to write with a Dictaphone, as did Oboler.) Media historians have established a link between these radio shows and the early television shows featuring celebrity hosts, one noting Robert Montgomery's appearances as host within the sets on the show that bore his name *Robert Montgomery Presents* (NBC, 1950–57) as a precursor of Serling's appearances on *The Twilight Zone* (Hey, 110–11).

Rod Serling teasing next week's episode, "The After Hours."

Sardonic host Raymond Edward Johnson of *Inner Sanctum* was also a precursor to the wave of late-night horror hosts that accompanied the release in 1957 of a package of classic Columbia and Universal thrillers and horror films, including *Frankenstein* (1931), *Dracula* (1931), and *Son of Frankenstein* (1939), known as *Shock Theatre* or *Shock!* A second package followed in 1959, the year *The Twilight Zone* began. Local stations airing the films were encouraged to have them introduced by "macabre masters of ceremonies," helping create such popular campy hosts as Zacherle (Philadelphia, New York), Morgus the Magnificent (New Orleans), and Ghoulardi (Cleveland). The *Shock Theatre* hosts "lent films an additional frisson of terror or a comic splash of camp" (Jowett and Abbott, 86). The most obvious example is, of course, Boris Karloff's *Thriller* (NBC, 1960–62), to which Karloff brought his considerable horror pedigree (he was the iconic Frankenstein's monster, after all). Serling's function as host must be understood within this tradition, although he was much too earnest to be campy, and his sartorial sharpness (with suits provided by Kuppenheimer and Eagle Clothes) seemed appropriate for *The Twilight Zone* and its focus on contemporary America.

For Sarah Kozloff, television hosts "serve to personalize the impersonal" (57). In the case of the speculative shows, though, the hosts served an additional function: like the anchors of news shows, these hosts "anchor" the speculations of their narrative in the real world, tethering them to the rational and the quotidian. Truman Bradley often said once he stepped before the camera, "Let me show you something interesting," after which he would offer a simple demonstration or experiment and then extrapolate from that to the "theme" of that night's episode. This anchoring function was important for both network executives and sponsors who, in the 1950s, were hesitant about prime-time shows that ventured into the fantastic.

The presentation of Rod Serling's teleplay "The Time Element," first broadcast on *The Westinghouse Desilu Playhouse* (CBS, 1958–60) on November 24, 1958, illustrates well this anchoring function of the host. The success of the "The Time Element" (the network received many letters praising the show) prompted CBS to begin serious discussions with Serling regarding his concept for *The Twilight Zone* (C. Serling 2009, 9). Serling later revisited the story's time-travel premise and the question of whether changing the past is possible in the *Twilight Zone* episode "Back There," in which a man (Russell Johnson) finds himself transported back to the evening when Abraham Lincoln is assassinated, a tragedy he is unable to prevent despite his foreknowledge—although his actions do alter the future in less profound ways.

As "The Time Element" begins, a disembodied narrator says, "Once upon a time there was a psychiatrist . . . ," immediately signaling that the narrative to follow will depart from realism and delve into the fantastic. Peter Jenson (William Bendix) comes to the office of a psychiatrist, Dr. Gillespie (Martin Balsam), with a strange story. Jenson is experiencing a recurring dream in which he is at Pearl Harbor shortly before the attack by the Japanese on December 7, 1941, and he believes that he is not merely dreaming but is in fact somehow going back seventeen years in time so that he can warn people of what is to come. However, in his dream he fails to convince anyone, and he always wakes up just before the bombs begin to fall. After listening to Jenson, Gillespie patiently explains the conventional paradoxes of time travel, which logically dictate that Jenson is experiencing a dream not reality, and despite Jenson's wish to discuss his problem "without dragging in Sigmund Freud," Gillespie offers his patient the textbook psychoanalytic explanation (not very different from that critical perspective regarding fantasy stories) that dreaming about altering the past is really a wish about changing something in the present.

The narrative of "The Time Element" ends ambiguously, with a twist that was to become characteristic of Serling's writing. While he is talking to Dr. Gillespie, Jenson finds himself at Pearl Harbor again, but now it is during the attack. As he looks out the windows of his hotel room, we hear the sound of low-flying aircraft, then the room explodes, followed by a cut to the psychiatrist, alone, with a disquieting feeling. Dr. Gillespie leaves his office and stops in for a drink at the local bar, where he sees a photograph of Jenson, who seems vaguely familiar to him. He asks the bartender (Jesse White) who the man is, and the bartender explains that Jenson was once also a bartender there but was killed at Pearl Harbor. Crucially, though, this episode of *The Westinghouse Desilu Playhouse* doesn't end here. After the story's conclusion, the show's host, Desi Arnaz, reappears and says he chooses a rational explanation over a fantastical one, that it was in fact all a dream on the part of the psychiatrist, who had seen the picture of Jenson on the wall in the bar some time previously. Serling's script leaves open the possibility of a fantastic explanation of events, while the celebrity host, a mainstream entertainer iconic of normative society, closes it down, eliminating any ambiguity with his preferred, officially sanctioned reading.

Apart from CBS's short-lived *'Way Out*, an anthology show featuring noted writer of the macabre Roald Dahl as host, which lasted for only fourteen episodes, Rod Serling was the only host of a network television show who was a writer rather than an actor. Of course, Serling was already something of a celebrity figure on television, a very successful writer interviewed on several talk shows before he made his first appearance on *The Twilight Zone*. After World War II, Serling attended Antioch College in Yellow Springs, Ohio, where he majored in English and gained experience writing for several radio and later television stations as part of his co-op work-study program. He sold his first script in 1949 (Grams, 5), and within a few years he was working as a freelance writer for early live nationally broadcast anthology shows such as *Kraft Television Theatre*, *Playhouse 90*, and *The Hallmark Hall of Fame* (*Hallmark Television Playhouse*: NBC 1951–78; CBS, 1979–81, 1982–89, 1995–2011; PBS, 1981; ABC 1989–95, 2011–14; Hallmark Channel, 2014), becoming famous for one in particular, "Patterns," a teleplay for *Kraft Television Theatre* about the power struggles and ethical dilemmas of several corporate executives. Broadcast on February 9, 1955, it became the first television drama to be repeated because of public demand, and because the original broadcast was live, the cast returned to perform the script again (Fiddy, 62). It won Serling the first of his six Emmy Awards, and a year later his script "Requiem for a Heavyweight" for *Playhouse 90*, about an over-the-hill boxer who is forced to compromise his integrity, earned him another as well as a Peabody Award, the first time this broadcasting award was given for writing (Zicree, 13). The first original ninety-minute show written specifically for television, "Requiem" also won Emmys for Best Direction, Best Performance, and Best Art Direction. Both of these scripts were subsequently adapted as feature films, *Patterns* in 1956 and *Requiem* in 1962.

A star writer, Serling was earning $10,000 per script for shows like *Playhouse 90* when in 1957 he decided to look for something different. As the writers of TV's "Golden Age" of live anthology drama—among them, Paddy Chayefsky, Robert Alan Aurthur, Tad Mosel, Reginald Rose, and Gore Vidal—were making the move to Hollywood while network television was shifting to filmed series and sitcoms, Serling bucked the trend and decided to stay with television. A chain-smoking workaholic, he was very prolific, turning out more than twenty original scripts in 1955 alone (Wright, 284). In 1959 he managed to write a book of short stories, three teleplays for *Playhouse 90*, rewrite a Broadway play, and produce twenty scripts for *The Twilight Zone* as well as supervising production of the show—all leading him to be diagnosed with physical exhaustion (Engel 193). The Young & Rubicam advertising agency, hired to help promote *The Twilight Zone*, thought Serling "the star" of a show that otherwise would have no reoccurring actors (Kraszweski, 353).

Serling's writing for *The Twilight Zone*, and sometimes elsewhere, follows a tradition of didactic fabulation that runs from Aesop to H. G. Wells, which he combined with a twist ending in the manner of O. Henry. Indeed, Serling, who earned a reputation as "O. Henry in Outer Space," adapted the earlier writer's story "Gift of the Magi" as a radio play while still in college (Engel, 187). The story tells of a husband and wife of modest means who independently sell something important to themselves in order to buy a Christmas present for the other, but both gifts turn out to be useless precisely because of what their spouse has sold. It concludes with the narrator suddenly announcing himself as such and drawing an explicit moral: "The magi, as you know, were wise men—wonderfully wise men—who brought gifts to the Babe in the manger. They invented the art of giving Christmas presents . . . And here I have lamely related to you the uneventful chronicle of two foolish children in a flat who most unwisely sacrificed for each other the greatest treasures of their house. But in a last word to the wise of these days let it be said that of all who give gifts these two were the wisest . . . They are the magi" (7). O. Henry's moral is that although neither gift turns out to have any practical value, both are beautiful expressions of the love the two have for each other—a sentiment Serling likely would have appreciated. Presnell and McGee see the episode "The Long Morrow" (5.15: January 10, 1964), in which an astronaut on an extended mission comes out of hibernation in order to be the same age as the woman he loves when he returns to Earth while unbeknownst to him she has placed herself in suspended animation, as an updating of O. Henry's story (173). Although they tend to be more dire, moral lessons analogous to those of O. Henry are to be found in many episodes of *The Twilight Zone*, and Serling's appearances, along with his opening and closing narrations, are similar to the sudden intrusion of O. Henry's authorial voice in the story.

Like Wells, Serling used the fantastic genres to offer moral lessons to a world filled with people less perfect than they should or could be. Serling explicitly refers to the twist of his own "The Rip Van Winkle Caper" (2.24: April 21, 1961), in which four thieves rob a train from Fort Knox filled with gold bullion and then hide in suspended animation for a hundred years only to emerge and discover that gold is worthless because it can now be synthesized, as "tonight's lesson—in the Twilight Zone." Similarly, at the end of "Nothing in the Dark" (3.16: January 5, 1962), after the elderly Wanda Dunn (Gladys Cooper) learns to accept the inevitability of death, Serling frames the story as an "object lesson for the more frightened amongst us." And the discovery by Professor Ellis Fowler (Donald Pleasence) of the important life lessons his teaching had brought his students over the years in "The Changing of the Guard" (3.37: June 1, 1962) Serling describes as "a very small scholastic lesson from the campus of the Twilight Zone." In "Night Call" Elva Keene (Gladys Cooper again) is "sadder, but wiser, by dint of a rather painful lesson in responsibility"; "In Praise of Pip" offers the "lesson" that "man is not as wise as he thinks." He concludes "Stopover in a Quiet Town" (5.30: April 24, 1964) by declaring that "the moral of what you've just seen is clear."

Fables typically feature anthropomorphized animals that dramatize their moral points, as with Joel Chandler Harris's Uncle Remus stories featuring Br'er Rabbit or George Orwell's *Animal Farm* (1945, originally subtitled "A Fairy Story"); *The Twilight Zone* stories substitute aliens, machines, and human caricatures in place of talking fauna. Serling biographer Gordon Sander refers to Serling as a "video Aesop," and Murray notes that "The Shelter" is a retelling in the atomic age of Aesop's fable of the grasshopper and the ant (Murray). Serling himself refers to the whimsical episode "Cavender is Coming" (3.36: May 25, 1962) as a fable, as he does "Hocus Pocus and Frisby" (3.30: April 13, 1962), about an inveterate blowhard (Andy Devine) who is briefly abducted by aliens but whom no one will believe, comparing it to Aesop's story about the boy who cried wolf.

Serling wrote more than half the scripts for *The Twilight Zone* (he was contractually bound to write 80 percent of them, whether original or adaptations) and acted as the show's executive producer. In June 1960, he also became the on-screen host, introducing the evening's episode and at the end teasing the next ("In a moment Rod Serling will return to tell you about next week's story"). In the first season Serling's opening narrations were done off-camera, and viewers didn't see him until the end of the episode, when he appeared to announce next week's installment. Also, beginning in the second season Serling is identified by the network voice as "the creator" of *The Twilight Zone*. The importance of his on-screen presence as host was crucial to the show (according to Colbert, "he introduced a whole generation to science fiction and chain smoking"). A number of other possible hosts were initially considered, including Westbrook Van Voorhis, who had been the authoritative voice of newsreel series *The March of Time* (1935–51), and the stentorian Orson Welles (Zicree, 24), who was already indelibly associated with science fiction because of his infamous Mercury Theatre on the Air radio adaptation of H. G. Wells's *War of the Worlds* broadcast on October 30, 1938.

Worland notes that Serling's presence at the beginning and end of each episode, along with his purplish narration, "is a powerful determinant of how one should interpret the tale" (104). For television scholar William Boddy, Serling's "stylized direct address and the frequently epigrammatic and moralistic closing voice-overs" emphasize his authorial signature, as does his sudden appearance in the space of the narrative (Boddy 1984, 107). This is true enough, although "the meaning" of Serling has been understood somewhat differently by different critics. On the one hand, Jon Kraszewski views Serling's presence as "intellectual" (354), while Worland sees Serling's "all-knowing grin" as signifying "the sage who comprehends more than the viewer but is willing to impart his wisdom to us if we only listen and observe" (104). Brian Murray writes that "He looked like a well-tailored young rabbi, upright but hip, delivering droll sermons through clenched teeth in a clipped and alliterative style" (Murray). According to the *New York Times*, on the other hand, Serling displayed "a facial expression of unusual intensity, combined with an anxiety to please, and just anxiety" (Grams, 95). CBS network executive and producer William Self thought Serling "brought to his hosting a kind of an 'everyman quality'" (Grams, 37)—very different from Kraszewski's and Worland view of him as an egghead. But apart from how we might read the nuances of Serling's presence on camera, certainly his pinched smile, suggesting a hint of irony, made him a perfect spokesman for the cruel turns of fate and inevitable comeuppances often meted out in the show's twist endings.

And, however we might understand the signification of Serling, his presence was so distinctive that he became inextricably associated with stranger things for the rest of his career. He edited several volumes of horror stories, including *Rod Serling's Triple W: Witches, Warlocks, and Werewolves* (1963), *Rod Serling's Devils and Demons* (1967), and *Rod Serling's Other*

Worlds (1978), his name always above the title. He introduced one episode of *Night Gallery* (NBC, 1969–1973), the show he hosted after *The Twilight Zone*, with "Good evening, sports fans. In discerning circles I'm known as the Howard Cosell of the crypt" (Murray). Western Publishing's long-running series of *Twilight Zone* comic books featured Serling as "host," his image superimposed over the cover art of each issue, for several years after his death, as if he were still hosting from the beyond.

In the denouement of the Western film *Saddle the Wind* (1958), scripted by Serling before *The Twilight Zone* launched, the town patriarch (Donald Crisp) tells the hero Steve Sinclair (Robert Taylor) that "I'm not going to moralize and tell you what happened is for the best." But Serling himself did this regularly in his writing, both for *The Twilight Zone* and other projects. In addition to this penchant for preaching, in *The Twilight Zone* (at least for the half-hour episodes) he followed the dictum regarding short fiction by Edgar Allan Poe, one of the major foundational figures of the fantastic. Poe's emphasis on the unity of a single effect—"In the whole composition there should be no word written of which the tendency, direct or indirect, is not to the one pre-established design" (Poe, 566)—clearly influenced Serling, as most *Twilight Zone* episodes build inexorably toward that narrative twist in the climax: the place of infinite abundance isn't heaven, but hell ("A Nice Place to Visit"); a megalomaniac astronaut lording it over tiny aliens is himself crushed by aliens in turn larger than he ("The Little People" [3.28: March 30, 1962]); and so on.*

The distinctive emphasis on the twist's moral lesson—submitted for our consideration—was characteristic of Serling's work, in *The Twilight Zone* as well as in his other film scripts, stories, and teleplays. Serling wrote the first screenplay draft

* Part of the reason the episodes in the fourth season are uniformly regarded as relatively weak is because at twice the length they diluted this unity of effect.

for the original *Planet of the Apes* film (1968), although subsequently it was heavily reworked by another writer, Michael Wilson, and the technologically advanced ape society Serling had envisioned was made more primitive at the suggestion of director Franklin J. Schaffner as a way to cut production costs. But the movie does retain Serling's twist ending, certainly one of the most famous in film history, in which we follow the astronaut Taylor (Charlton Heston) as he travels along the shoreline of the Forbidden Zone and eventually comes upon the ruins of the Statue of Liberty and realizes, along with the audience, that he has been on Earth in the future all along and not on another planet. Pierre Boulle's novel on which the film was based also has a twist ending, but a rather different one: in Boulle's novel the narrative is a written document found floating in space by a vacationing astronaut couple who, we now learn, are chimpanzees who dismiss the entire account as preposterous before heading for home. (Interestingly, in the first-season *Twilight Zone* episode "People Are Alike All Over," written by Serling, Roddy McDowall, who would star in four of the five original Apes movies as Cornelius, plays an astronaut who is treated kindly by aliens—only to discover that he is considered a lower form of life and so has been confined in a "natural habitat" like an animal in a zoo—the same way Taylor is treated in *Planet of the Apes*.)

Serling once explained that "I began producing so I could write for myself, have a hand in the casting, and meet sponsors on their own ground" (Grams, 18). This is true enough, but, of course, while Serling's approach and vision profoundly shaped the show, he wasn't solely responsible for its quality and achievements. Even with the scripts Serling wrote, not all were original; some were adapted from the work of established science-fiction writers such as Jerome Bixby ("It's a Good Life") and Damon Knight ("To Serve Man"). He adapted scripts from anthologies, mainstream magazines, the science-fiction pulps, and even from a radio play ("The Hitch-Hiker"). Ray Bradbury adapted his own story "I Sing the Body Electric" (3.35: May 18, 1962) and was supposed to have been more involved in writing for the show, but disputes with Serling over intellectual property seem to have prevented that from happening. (During the show's run, plagiarism lawsuits were filed over six of Serling's scripts, all of which were settled out of court.) For the scripts Serling didn't write himself, he relied mostly on two writers who had attended a meeting and screening of the pilot episode, Richard Matheson and Charles Beaumont. The two men were friends, and both were excited about the prospect of writing for *The Twilight Zone*.

Matheson, who would write fourteen episodes and had two others adapted from his stories by Serling, had established his reputation as a writer of horror and science fiction. Many of Matheson's stories and novels have been adapted (mostly by himself) for film, among them *The Shrinking Man* (1956, filmed in 1959 as *The Incredible Shrinking Man*) and *A Stir of Echoes* (1958, film version 1999). His postapocalyptic novel *I Am Legend* (1954), a major influence on George A. Romero's *Night of the Living Dead* (1968), has been adapted to film four times (*The Last Man on Earth* [1964], *The Omega Man* [1971], *I Am Legend* [2007], and *I Am Omega* [2007]). Beaumont, author of twenty-two episodes (two episodes credited to him were ghost-written by others when he became too ill to write), more than any other writer after Serling, had published stories in *Playboy* magazine, published a collection of his fiction entitled *The Hunger and Other Stories* (1957), and had written the screenplay for *Queen of Outer Space* (1958) starring Zsa Zsa Gabor (intended, he claimed, as a parody but not quite filmed that way). While writing for *The Twilight Zone*, Beaumont, like Serling a prolific writer, was also writing scripts for a variety of other shows, such as *Have Gun—Will Travel* and *Richard Diamond, Private Detective* (CBS, 1957–59; NBC, 1959–60) as well as *One Step Beyond* and *Thriller*. By all accounts a man of extraordinary energy, Beaumont became ill at thirty-four with what was possibly Alzheimer's or Pick's disease or a combination of the two. He died four years later, his only other important contribution to the macabre being the screenplay for Roger Corman's *The Masque of the Red Death* (1964), regarded by many as the best movie by the prolific filmmaker known as the King of the Bs.

Buck Houghton, who had worked as a production assistant on several of Val Lewton's classic horror films (*The Curse of the Cat People* [1944], *The Body Snatcher* [1945], *Bedlam* [1946]), served as producer for the first three seasons of the show, working harmoniously with Serling and director of photography George T. Clemens, a seasoned cinematographer for Paramount who shot more than half the episodes of *The Twilight Zone*. Houghton was hired to coproduce the show in order to give Serling more time to write. The producer readily acknowledges that "*The Twilight Zone* was shaped by Rod Serling" (Houghton, 10), yet, according to Zicree, Houghton was responsible for everything "from the purchasing of scripts (other than Serling's) to casting to scoring to cutting" (30). His work ranged from approving budgets and contracts to approving shooting locations and sets, Houghton left after the third season, accepting another producing position because of the uncertainty over continued sponsorship for *The Twilight Zone* and a reluctance to work on the one-hour episodes, which he felt worked against the show ("I told them that *Twilight Zone* is based on a willing suspension of disbelief. You can't ask people to do it for an hour" [qtd. in Engel, 232]).

How is it that these various and disparate people could produce a weekly show that had any consistency of style or vision? Bruce Kawin has offered a helpful modification of the classic conception of the auteur theory, which viewed the film director as artist solely responsible for the work we see on the screen, to take into account the collaborative realities of the production process in film and, by extension, television. Because movies and television shows are the result of many individuals working together, Kawin compares the director to an orchestra conductor: "The instrument that a conductor plays is, in fact, the orchestra. The orchestra members depend on the conductor to keep time and to let them know when and with what emphasis to play. The conductor organizes the performance, and it is therefore up to her or him how the composition will be realized" (Kawin, 190). Thus, Kawin argues, we may view auteurist works as the result not of top-down decisions on various production aspects imposed by the auteur (usually the director) but rather, of what he calls "collaboration as a system" in which the various individuals involved in a production work together toward a shared vision (197–99).

If, for example, individuals were working on a John Huston film, they sought to provide what they thought would be needed for a "Huston film," a group concept rather than an individual one: "They each do their part, and the parts are coherent because they were each fashioned in relation to an ideal of the whole" (Kawin, 198). This seemed to be the way that *The Twilight Zone* was realized. Certainly, Beaumont and Matheson, both of whom tended to approach the fantastic by putting recognizable, everyday characters in strange situations, fit comfortably with Serling's concern with the moral behavior of the average man. It is not surprising, therefore, that the show, as is uniformly agreed, suffered a decline in quality after the first three seasons, when Serling became less involved in production aspects and Houghton left and was replaced by Herbert Hirschman (and later Bert Granet), whose views of the fantastic did not quite sync with Serling's (Grams, 124).

In some cases we may hypothesize that a particular director was assigned to a specific episode because they had some affinity for the subject: Robert Florey with the noirish "Perchance to Dream" and the overheated "The Fever," John Brahm with "Judgment Night" and "The Four of Us Are Dying," Mitchell Leisen with "The Sixteen-Millimeter Shrine" (1.4: October 23, 1959), Jacques Tourneur with "Night Call," Ida Lupino with "The Masks," veteran comedy director Norman Z. McLeod with "Once upon a Time." Elsewhere I have read the "Uncle Simon" episode within the context of Don Siegel's other films, especially *Invasion of the Body Snatchers* (Grant 2010, 43–49). But it is also the case that, as written, "Uncle Simon" is a typical Serling morality tale with a narrative twist at the end that suggests once again the irony of poetic justice for a venal and vindictive character. The plot involves an irascible, rancorous old man (Sir Cedric Hardwicke) and his repressed and bitter niece Barbara Polk (Constance Ford), who tends slavishly to his excessive demands but is only waiting for him to die in order to inherit his ample estate as recompense for the constant abuse she has endured. After Uncle Simon suffers an accidental fall that breaks his back, Barbara offers no assistance when she realizes he is dying. And so she comes into his estate—with the proviso in his will that she must care for his last experiment. The experiment turns out to be a robot of himself invented by Uncle Simon, a slightly modified Robby the Robot from *Forbidden Planet* but here with Uncle Simon's grating voice and unctuous personality. Just as we might read something of Siegel's concern with emotional alienation in "Uncle Simon," so we may also understand it as a Serling morality tale. Here, as elsewhere, personal directorial touches or themes do not preclude reading an episode of the show as being consistent with expressing aspects of Serling's overarching vision as well.

Undoubtedly, the episode most celebrated for its imaginative visuals is "Eye of the Beholder," written by Serling and directed by Douglas Heyes. In the story, Janet Tyler (Maxine Stuart [under bandages] / Donna Douglas [after bandages removed]), whose face is horribly disfigured, is in the hospital awaiting the results of her final allowable attempt at corrective surgery. If the surgery is unsuccessful, by law she will become an outcast, exiled to an isolated community of similarly repulsive-looking people. The episode is shot in such a way (lighting and shadow, over-the-shoulder shots and subjective point-of-view shots, blocking, and framing) so that we never see the characters' faces—until the twist climax, when Janet's bandages are finally removed and we discover that the faces of the doctors and nurses are horribly distorted while the protagonist is, from our perspective, conventionally beautiful (Donna Douglas would go on to play Elly Mae Clampett in *The Beverly Hillbillies*). Heyes and George Clemens worked together to choreograph the blocking of actors and camera movements "as meticulously as a ballet" (Zicree, 148) so that the design does not become obvious and give away the twist beforehand. The heavy reliance on shadows, appropriate to the dark and foreboding atmosphere of the story, and the canny high-angle shots looking down on Janet and the medical staff in her hospital room evoke, once again, film noir and seem to work as an expression of the entrapping nature of enforced conformity and thus "justify" its expressionist style. In addition to being another of Serling's warnings about conformity, the episode's moral lesson is that standards of beauty are socially determined, hence relative and subjective, so that we should not shun people who are different—again, consistent with the show's emphasis, as discussed more fully in the next chapter, on the importance of and challenges to democratic individualism. Thus, even the most visually stylized of episodes still conforms to the show's paradigmatic approach of moral fabulation tinged with irony.

Discussing the use of popular music in the show to enhance the sense of nostalgia in Serling's scripts about attempts to return to the past, musicologist Reba Wissner observes that the same treatment informs those episodes about the past written by others and explains this as likely the result of Serling choosing the scripts that appealed to his own interests (60). This is probably so, but it is also the case that the regular production unit for *The Twilight Zone* was extraordinarily cohesive, encouraging that dynamic of "collaboration as a system." According to CBS producer William Self, most of the crew working on the show, including cameraman Clemens and production manager Ralph W. Nelson, had worked together before for Meridian Productions's *Schlitz Playhouse of Stars* (CBS, 1951–59) (Grams 51), so they already had an established working relationship when

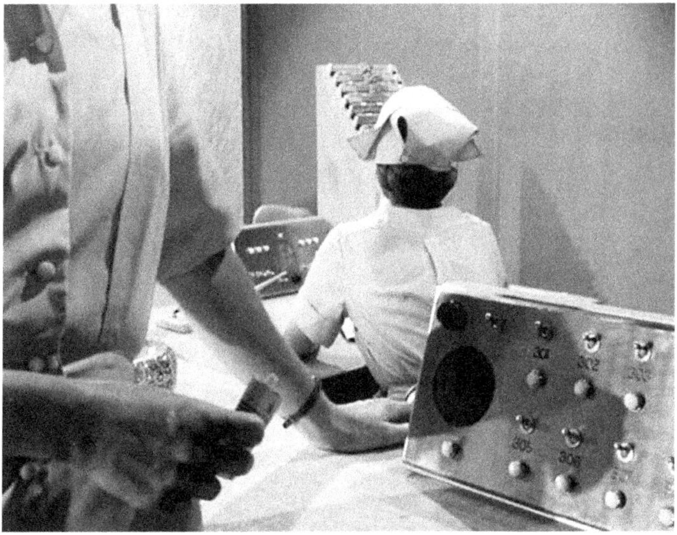

The choreography of the camera and actors in "Eye of the Beholder."

they came to *The Twilight Zone*. Many of the production personnel carried over from season to season.*

Of the several noted writers of television's "Golden Age" of live television drama in the mid-1950s, only Serling maintained an important presence in television as the medium transitioned into the series format (Boddy 1984, 98). John Newland directed all the episodes of *One Step Beyond* as well as hosted the show, but Serling was the only writer to find true celebrity success as a series host. According to television scholar Jane M. Shattuc, "Applying the concept of the 'author' or 'artist' to television is always difficult, but it is particularly thorny when applied to American television" (143). Serling, though, clearly was a television auteur well before,

* The names of all crew members for each season are listed in Grams, "Appendix A: Production Credits," 719–22.

say, Norman Lear or Steven Bochco or any of today's lauded showrunners. Serling, who wrote or adapted ninety-two of the show's 156 episodes, was undeniably "the creator" and auteur of *The Twilight Zone*.

But it was authorship with a difference from the classical notion of the auteur in cinema. In a foundational essay for what would become the auteur theory, French critic Alexandre Astruc imagined cinema developing as an art to the point that the camera would function like a pen ("la caméra stylo") for a writer and that the image would "become a means of writing just as flexible and subtle as written language" (18). Later, Gore Vidal argued that fellow television writer Paddy Chayefksy was an auteur who used different directors as his "pencil" (153), and something similar may be said about Serling, who used *The Twilight Zone*'s crew, directors, and writers like a box of crayons to provide various shadings to his basic vision. This worldview, essentially a conflicted view of bourgeois individualism, is explored in more detail in the next chapter.

3

"What's in the Box"

The Twilight Zone and the Real World

Rod Serling touted *The Twilight Zone* as a vehicle for prospective advertisers to sell their products, yet at the same time he complained about artistic compromise, "which in essence is what the television writer does if he wants to put on controversial themes" (qtd. in Zicree, 96). In a 1974 speech to the American Advertising Federation, Serling mused that "You wonder how to put on a meaningful drama that is adult, incisive probing when every fifteen minutes the proceedings are interrupted by twelve dancing rabbits with toilet paper" (Murray). Yet, according to Murray, five years earlier, in the two years 1968 and 1969 alone, Serling himself appeared in ads selling an astonishing array of goods and services, among them Crest toothpaste, Goodrich radial tires, Westinghouse appliances, Anacin, Samsonite luggage, and Volkswagens. Already in the first season of *The Twilight Zone* Kimberly-Clark, a paper-products company, wanted to insert a product ad in the corner of the screen during the closing credits (Grams, 59)—a wish Serling and Buck Houghton successfully resisted, at least temporarily. In the fifth and last season of the show, the images of Pall Mall cigarettes or Lilt hair shampoo did appear alongside the credits, a graphic statement of the show's balance of art and commerce and the middle ground ("between light and shadow"?) that Serling as executive producer inevitably accepted.

In the episode "Static," written by Charles Beaumont, Ed Lindsay (Dean Jagger) flees the modern horrors of television for old broadcasts on his antique radio. One of the annoying commercials he hears on television is for "Green" cigarettes: "Green, cool grass, the touch, the smell of green, cool grass, now brought to you for the first time in Green, the new chlorophyll cigarette, the smoke that doesn't smell like tobacco, but smells good, green, cool, like grass . . ." At the end of a few episodes, at the prodding of Liggett & Myers, Serling, a heavy smoker in real life, appears to tell us about next week's episode while holding a cigarette, once or twice even plugging Chesterfield or Oasis cigarettes, two of L&M's brands. He was perhaps choking on the smoke literally as well as metaphorically as he displayed a pack in the palm of his hand and said, "Here's an item we forgot. You see this? It holds a promise for anyone who smokes. It's Oasis. And as its name implies, it promises you the most refreshing, softest taste of all. Try Oasis—I think you'll like it."

In the show's first season, General Foods signed on as primary sponsor, and Kimberly-Clark, manufacturer of such brands as Kleenex, Kotex, and Scotties among others, agreed to be alternate sponsor. After the initial sponsorship of twenty-six episodes, General Foods hesitantly renewed its sponsorship, but Kimberly-Clark did not, and CBS eventually signed on Colgate-Palmolive for the second season. In the third season Liggett & Myers Tobacco Company replaced General Foods, in turn followed later by Procter & Gamble. During the hour-long episodes of the fourth season, which allowed for more advertising, additional sponsorship was provided by Johnson & Johnson, US Royal tires, and Pepsi-Cola. By the time *The Twilight Zone* had finished its five-year run, the panoply of other products that had sponsored it included Sanka coffee; Crest toothpaste, Rise Shave Cream, and Arrid roll-on deodorant; Contac decongestant and Bufferin aspirin; Prell and Halo shampoos; and Tareyton, Oasis, and Chesterfield cigarettes.

In the fall of the second season, six episodes of *The Twilight Zone* were shot on videotape rather than on film as a cost-saving measure, a budgetary decision that compromised the look of the show significantly. The videotaped episodes saved 10 percent of production costs because videotape could be edited directly, without waiting for dailies. But this production method precluded the possibility of location shooting.* Before then, shooting on location in, for example, Death Valley had contributed substantially to the arid atmosphere and feeling of desperation in "The Lonely" and "I Shot an Arrow into the Air" (1.15: January 15, 1960), while both "A Hundred Yards over the Rim" and "The Rip Van Winkle Caper" were filmed in Lone Pine, California, the areas' open horizons, sand dunes, and distinctive light central to all. By contrast, the sets in the videotaped episodes look mostly—unsurprisingly—like uninspired sets. The desultory used-car lot in "The Whole Truth," for example, is clearly an interior set without a whiff of the outdoors about it. Also, the videotaped episodes were transferred to 16 mm film for broadcast, inevitably losing definition in the process. Serling himself felt that the videotape experiment was a "disastrous" compromise because it was "neither fish nor fowl. You're bound to the same kind of natural laws as in live TV, but they try to mix it with certain qualities of film" (Zicree, 194).

Other small commercial concessions and changes found their way into episodes. For example, in his original script for the episode "Judgment Night," Serling had the ship's first officer ask for tea to be brought to the bridge, but General Foods, makers of Sanka coffee, took exception, and so the line was changed to ordering "a tray" (Zicree, 52). Concerns from the network required Serling to make some changes to the script

* The six episodes were "The Lateness of the Hour," "Static," "The Whole Truth," "Night of the Meek," "Twenty-Two," and "Long-Distance Call."

Location photography in Death Valley enhances the arid atmosphere of "The Lonely."

for "He's Alive" as well, altering the fascist group's logo from a swastika to a hand gripping a torch accompanied by a lightning bolt (Presnell and McGee, 142). In Serling's original teleplay for "Uncle Simon," the odious uncle was depicted as a pipe smoker, a habit carried over in the robot replacement, but the sponsor at the time, the American Tobacco Company, had it deleted and replaced by hot chocolate (Zicree, 312). More importantly, the network also imposed a scheduling change in the fourth season that forced it to expand from its original half-hour slot on Friday nights from 10:00 to 10:30 p.m. to an hour slot on Thursdays from 9:00 to 10:00 p.m. before moving back again. During the summer of 1960, when Serling was filling in as a temporary columnist for the *New York Herald Tribune*, he responded to a reader's question "Are writers' complaints about TV censorship and sponsorship interference valid?" by writing,

"Censorship and intrusion are more the rule in television than the exception" (Grams, 82).

In a television interview Mike Wallace conducted with Serling in 1959, just days before the debut of *The Twilight Zone*, Serling explained that he was tired of stupid fights with sponsors, such as when the line "Got a match?" in his "Requiem for a Heavyweight" script was struck because the sponsor of *Playhouse 90* was Ronson, a manufacturer of cigarette lighters (Grams, 18; Zicree, 14). Serling vented these frustrations in several *Twilight Zone* episodes, none more explicitly than in "The Bard," an hour-long episode devoted almost wholly to comic swipes at commercial television that barely hide the bitterness toward what he called the "Mount Sinai of Advertisers Row" (qtd. in Hunt, 10). The story's main character, the boorish and untalented Julius Moomer (Jack Weston), is a former streetcar conductor and now aspiring writer (his dream of winning the "Wurlitzer Prize" reveals how little he knows about literature) who, researching black magic for the pilot for a new horror/fantasy series ("black magic, conjuring, that sort of thing"), manages to conjure the ghost of William Shakespeare (British actor John Williams) as his literal ghostwriter. Before the distinguished playwright's arrival, we get a sense of Moomer's writing abilities when he pitches absurd formula stories (with twists!) to his agent, who unenthusiastically tells him, "I've never heard so many varieties of the same story." Fred Steiner's music for the episode associates Moomer and formula television with carnival barkers, and in a seemingly digressive bit of comic business, Burt Reynolds's mildly funny parody of Marlon Brando in *A Streetcar Named Desire* anticipates the media-studies concept that television's continual flow, as initially formulated by media scholar Raymond Williams, manages to turn even once-shocking realism into triviality.

Moomer decides not to waste Shakespeare on a mere pilot and instead has him write a dramatic teleplay, portentously entitled "The Tragic Cycle," that network executives think they

Shakespeare (John Williams) meets Tennessee Williams (Burt Reynolds as Rocky Rhodes) in "The Bard."

like ("it has imagery," concedes one) and want to produce for "Shannon Playhouse." They are a little hesitant because the language, for some reason they cannot fathom, tends toward the archaic, like Elizabethan English, so "sponsor-wise, the thing requires some noodling." Soon the sponsors and network executives make wholesale changes to the script, completely altering it ("like a roomful of butchers at work on a steer"), the changes determined by the principle that television needs to speak to the hypothetical "lady in Dubuque." Moomer nervously agrees to all of them (including deleting the big love scene on the balcony because people don't have balconies anymore). When he sucks up to the boorish Mr. Shannon (John McGiver), president of the show's sponsoring company, by telling him that he loves Shannon's onion soup, the latter angrily insists that they don't make it because onion soup is French and Shannon Foods is a proud, wholly American company (such comic business seems less absurd after the post-9/11 idea of "Freedom Fries").

Serling's feelings about the rat race of commercialism is also clear in two earlier episodes, among the series' best, "Walking Distance" and "A Stop at Willoughby," both original teleplays by Serling in the first season featuring advertising executives in their thirties (roughly the same age as the author at the time) who are disillusioned with the pressures of modern urban life and who long for an idyllic pastoral past. Unlike the acerbic "The Bard," both episodes are infused with a deep sense of nostalgia. Others have noted the autobiographical connection in these stories in that the towns depicted evoke those of the Finger Lakes district of Serling's own boyhood. (In his final interview, in response to a question regarding what time period he would prefer to live in, he said "Victorian times. Small town. Bandstands. Summer" [Brevelle].) Serling nodded to the area with the name of his production company, Cayuga Productions, and upstate New York explicitly figures as a location in several episodes. In "Walking Distance" Martin Sloan (Gig Young)—"vice-president, ad agency, in charge of media," Serling informs us in his introduction—while out for a drive in the country finds he has somehow gone back in time to the town of his youth. He rushes to see his parents, who reject him as crazy, although his father (Frank Overton) eventually believes him and convinces the grown-up Martin to return to his own time because that past belongs to his boyhood self whom he sees happily playing in a park. Martin assents to his father's wisdom and returns the way he arrived, realizing that one cannot dwell in the past.

In the darker "Willoughby" the pressures of advertising and all the commercialism it entails prove too much for Gart Williams (James Daly), a man, as Serling tells us, "protected by a suit of armor all held together by one bolt" that is about to be removed. The pressures of his job together with an unsupportive and materialistic wife and a gnawing ulcer nudge Williams to fall asleep on his nightly train commute home and to dream about a charming, archetypal nineteenth-century American town ("July, midsummer, 1888," Serling tells us at the beginning) that apparently does not exist on the route. Reaching the breaking point, Williams decides that next time the town appears he will get off in Willoughby, a place, the train conductor explains, "where a man can slow down to a walk and live his life full measure." In the twist ending, after Williams departs the train when it next stops at Willoughby, there is a cut to the conductor and a trainman standing outside the stopped train in a snowstorm discussing the fact that Williams had suddenly jumped off the moving train and was killed instantly. The authorities have been contacted, Williams's body is loaded into a hearse, and as the door is closed, we see in close-up the sign on it: "Willoughby Funeral Home."

Directed by experienced Hollywood director, editor, and actor Robert Parrish, who also directed *Saddle the Wind*, "Willoughby" features several noteworthy visual touches. The imaginary town, which Williams dreams about three times, is photographed in bright, inviting sunlight, offering a bold contrast to the snowy blackness enveloping the train car before Williams falls asleep. The first time the train "arrives" in Willoughby, the town is shown in long shot with its American flag on the pole, a man riding by on a penny-farthing bicycle, and two boys in straw hats with fishing poles like Huck Finn and Tom Sawyer. The second time, we see also a classic bandstand in the town park. Williams tells his wife that the town looks like a Currier and Ives painting—to which she coldly responds by complaining that she married a man whose big dream is to be Huckleberry Finn. (The reference is evoked again in the final episode of the show, "The Bewitchin' Pool," in which two children escape their stern, bickering parents by discovering a wonderfully harmonious world at the bottom of the family swimming pool—in their imaginations, "floating down a raft like Tom Sawyer.")

The episode's other visual contrast involves a bold use of the close-up, emphasized in television style generally but here, as often in *The Twilight Zone*, given special expressive

The town from the past beckons in "A Stop at Willoughby."

significance. During an executive meeting early on, Williams's feeling of the mounting pressure on him is summed up in the big close-ups of the mouth of his boss, Mr. Misrell (Howard Smith), a cigar jammed in it as he bellows "Push, push, push. All the way. All the time." Shots alternate between Misrell's bellowing and Williams wincing in pain from his ulcer, each of the three successive shots of Misrell's face tighter until the screen is filled with just his barking mouth. The episode also uses close-ups, this time of Williams's face, to signal the transitions from wintry modern train car to old-fashioned one in summer. The slight discontinuity in the cuts between the close-ups of each transition suggests the radical shift from quotidian reality to the imaginary world of Willoughby.

Before taking his last, fateful train ride, Williams finally cracks in the office while calls on two different telephones and his secretary all demand his attention at the same time, perhaps mirroring Serling's feelings about the competing demands of art and commerce in the medium of television. Serling told Mike Wallace that he thinks it is possible still to produce adult drama on television, that television can be "commercial" and meaningful at the same time, that it can attain both public acceptance and artistic merit. But it was a difficult balancing act, and it took a toll on him. "Walking Distance" and "Willoughby" are similar on a narrative level, as both protagonists desire to escape the demands of the present by fleeing to a happier time in the past. But while the protagonist of "Walking Distance," although wistfully nostalgic, accepts that it is impossible to return to the time of one's youth, that of "Willoughby" is unable to come to terms with his present life, and for him the only resolution is through death. This striking difference between the two episodes, both coming in the first season, mirrors Serling's own ambivalence about television and his work in it.*

On another level, Misrell's "Push, push" also may be understood to refer to the dynamics of capitalist competition more generally, not just to the advertising business that fuels its desire. Douglas Brode points out that in "Walking Distance" Martin's last name, Sloan, evokes that of Sloan Wilson, author of the 1955 best-seller *The Man in the Gray Flannel Suit*, about another corporate executive and conflicted commuter (5). To be sure, in addressing contemporary issues at all, *The Twilight Zone* moved away from the juvenile nature of such earlier television science-fiction shows as *Captain Video and His Video Rangers* (DuMont, 1949–54), *Tom Corbett, Space Cadet* (all four networks, 1950–55), *Space Patrol* (ABC, 1950–55), and *Rocky Jones, Space Ranger* (1954), but ultimately, it cannot be said that the show offered any sustained critique of capitalism. Indeed,

* One of Serling's scripts for *Playhouse 90*, "The Velvet Alley," which was broadcast in January the same year *The Twilight Zone* debuted, is a semiautobiographical drama about the seductiveness of Hollywood ("the velvet alley") and a television writer (Art Carney) who gets his big break.

Mr. Misrell barks his orders in close-up in "A Stop at Willoughby."

overall the show's political messages were conflicted, a conflict that was itself symptomatic of the capitalist system of which it was a part.

The late episode "I Am the Night—Color Me Black" (5.26: March 27, 1964), written by Serling, is one of the show's most overt message episodes. The story takes place in an unnamed American town—so vaguely depicted as to be Anywhere, USA—where a man named Jagger (Terry Becker) is about to be executed for murder after a rigged trial (elements of the Emmett Till story resurfacing here). That morning the sun does not rise, and an inexplicable blackness descends upon the town. There is no twist ending to this episode—indeed, no narrative closure at all—just the darkness closing in on the town and, as we learn, elsewhere around the world in other, real places where hate is also happening: Birmingham, the Berlin Wall, and Vietnam. The episode hints toward a racial theme: the victim is described as a "cross-burning, psychopathic bully," and the method of execution is public hanging, although in this case the person to be hung is white. In the episode "pretentious writing overwhelms fine acting" (Zicree, 409) as the story turns entirely on one obvious and belabored metaphor. Serling punches home his point in his final comment by observing that this phenomenon is to be found in the real world, not in *The Twilight Zone*: "A sickness known as hate; not a virus, not a microbe, not a germ—but a sickness nonetheless, highly contagious, deadly in its effects. Don't look for it in the Twilight Zone—look for it in a mirror. Look for it before the light goes out altogether." Perhaps because the show was shortly to be going off the air, Serling felt sufficiently emboldened to abandon the protective mantle of fantasy almost completely to offer this most pointed screed regarding his fellow Americans.

"I Am the Night" was first telecast at a time not only when civil-rights demonstrations were gaining momentum but also when substantial escalation of US involvement in the Vietnam conflict was occurring (the Gulf of Tonkin Resolution, the act that provided the legal basis for American escalation, was passed by Congress in August 1964, just three months after "I Am the Night" was telecast), although most Americans were still unaware of the country's dangerously increasing entanglement in that remote South Asian country. Just six months earlier, in the September 1963 episode "In Praise of Pip" a title card tells us that the opening location is a jungle in Vietnam, after which a soldier's father (Jack Klugman) proclaims, "My kid is dying. In a place called South Vietnam . . . There isn't even supposed to be a war going on there, and my son is dying." Some writers have suggested that this is the first mention of the Vietnam War in a television drama (Grams, 607). Still, despite these references, with few exceptions *The Twilight Zone* only infrequently addressed the particulars of then-current events directly.

Historical events sometimes informed specific episodes: the assassination of Lincoln ("Back There"), Nazi Germany ("The

Obsolete Man"). The Holocaust is confronted in "Death's-Head Revisited" (3.9: November 10, 1961) by a former SS captain (Oscar Beregi) visiting Dachau who is driven insane by the ghosts of those he killed. Serling concludes the episode telling us that the concentration camps "must remain standing" because "the moment we forget this, the moment we cease to be haunted by its remembrance, then we become the gravediggers. Something to dwell on and remember, not only in the Twilight Zone but wherever men walk God's Earth." In "The Chaser" an embarrassed Roger Shackleforth, avoiding the real reason for his visit to the alchemist A. Daemon (John McIntire), observes that the current situation in China is "ugly"—to which the alchemist replies "You don't look so good yourself," a joke that points to the show's preference for the politics of the personal.

One episode, though, did unambiguously respond to contemporary events—"The Mirror," featuring Peter Falk as Ramos Clemente, a rebel who seizes power in an unnamed Central American country. The leader he deposes tells Clemente that a magical mirror in the palace office will show him the face of his assassins. Ramos soon sees some of his fellow rebels in the glass, grows increasingly paranoid, and begins a wave of executions, ultimately becoming like the tyrant he had deposed. In the end, Clemente, who is made up to look unmistakably like Fidel Castro with military fatigues, beard, and cigar, sees his own reflection in the mirror and kills himself. The episode's moral is basically that absolute power corrupts absolutely and that Castro is a perfect example. The Cuban leader's visit to New York in September 1960, and his speech at the UN General Assembly in which he denounced imperialism and colonialism, was widely covered in the press at the time, just a year before the episode was aired in October 1961. But in case we have missed the portrait, Serling closes the episode by remarking that "any resemblance to tyrants living or dead is hardly coincidental." The episode promises some complexity in its portrait of Ramos because, as Worland notes, he begins as a sympathetic character with an idealistic cause (107–8), but quickly its depiction of Clemente reduces the revolutionary Marxism Castro represents to personal psychopathology. Presnell and McGee's assessment that any viewer knowing Woody Allen's *Bananas* (1971) would find it difficult to watch "The Mirror" without laughing may be somewhat harsh, but like other episodes that share with it the aim of examining the dictatorial impulse—"The Obsolete Man," "The Little People," "Four O'Clock" (3.29: April 6, 1962)—it reduces ideology to the inevitable corruption of one man's will to power while at the same time stripping a Marxist alternative to capitalism of any serious ideological basis.

A slightly more nuanced political lesson is offered in the comic fantasy episode "The Whole Truth," also written by Serling. In this episode sleazy car salesman Harvey Hunnicut (Jack Carson) finds himself, after hustling a customer for his antique

Revolutionary leader Ramos Clemente (Peter Falk) sees his enemies in "The Mirror."

Model A for much less than its value, with a cursed vehicle that forces its owner to tell the truth. As a consequence, Hunnicut is unable to sell a single vehicle because he admits everything that is wrong with each of them to potential buyers. In the whimsical conclusion he manages to sell the car to Nikita Khrushchev to use as a propaganda tool to display the poor state of American technology and lifestyle to his own people. The final shot shows the barely glimpsed face of an actor resembling the Soviet premier smiling with that peculiarly capitalist pride of ownership as he is driven off the lot in the cursed car. The viewer may chuckle with the realization that now Khrushchev will have to tell the truth, meaning there will be no more Communist propaganda and that the Iron Curtain will eventually crumble. The episode acknowledges the ideological tensions between the world's two superpowers but then reassuringly dismisses the threat of Communism as nothing but a lie and the butt of the episode's joke while endorsing the American entrepreneurial ethic. Still, one might be left uneasy with the implication that it will take nothing less than magic to win the Cold War.

Cold War fears loom over *The Twilight Zone*, the threat of the atomic bomb informing specific episodes as well as the show's overall feeling of anxiety. J. Hoberman points out that the episode "The Midnight Sun" (3.10: November 17, 1961), about two women waiting to die as the Earth has left its orbit and is heading toward the sun, was broadcast on the same day that the US successfully launched its first Minuteman intercontinental ballistic missile (ICBM); in this context, Serling's opening narration ("Even at midnight, it's high noon—the hottest day in history") takes on an immediate ominousness (51). "The Shelter," an episode that, like "I Am the Night," shows Serling's writing at its most strident—"Rod in one of his messianic moods," observed the episode's director, Lamont Johnson (Zicree, 227)—was aired between the Bay of Pigs disaster in August and the Cuban Missile Crisis in October (Mortenson, 72). The story begins with a group of neighbors gathered to celebrate the birthday of

Dr. Stockton (Larry Gates), a physician who has tended to their families over the years, even delivering some of their children. Good cheer exudes all around—until a radio message (the contemporaneous CONELRAD warning system is mentioned specifically) announces that radar has picked up some unidentified incoming objects that could be missiles. The group disperses as the families leave to prepare for the attack, but they all return shortly thereafter because the Stocktons are the only family on the block with the foresight to have built a fallout shelter. They all plead with Dr. Stockton to let them in, but he refuses because the shelter only has supplies and air sufficient for his own family. As the time ticks down until the missiles arrive, the other families become increasingly desperate and hysterical, attacking each other and in their frenzy breaking down the door of the shelter to get in, thus making it unusable for anyone. As they storm through the broken door, an announcement comes over the radio indicating that the mysterious objects have now been identified as satellites and that there is no danger. The neighbors then try to regain their civilized demeanor, but Dr. Stockton ascends the basement staircase so that, lecturing down to his embarrassed friends (and the audience), he delivers the episode's ironic point: "We were spared a bomb tonight, but I wonder if we weren't destroyed even without it."

The episode perhaps most frequently discussed by critics for its politics is "The Monsters Are Due on Maple Street," another cautionary Cold War tale in which aliens conquer humankind by manipulating average Americans' innate fear of the Other to the point that they destroy themselves. Maple Street at first seems like suburban bliss in another Anytown, USA: as the episode begins, men are washing cars and pruning bushes in their front yards, kids are playing baseball and buying ice cream. Suddenly something passes overhead accompanied by an electronic hum and flash of light. When the power on the street goes out and the neighbors gather, young Tommy (Jan Handzlik), his imagination spurred by the SF pulps he reads, suggests that

Dr. Stockton (Larry Gates) as the moral conscience in "The Shelter."

aliens are invading and that in all the stories he's read there are advance scouts hidden among humankind. The idea planted, people become increasingly suspicious of each other while the level-headed Steve (Claude Akins) tries to keep everyone calm; but the impulsive Charlie Farnsworth (Jack Weston) grabs a rifle and shoots at an approaching sound that turns out to be a neighbor, Pete Van Horn (Ben Erway), returning in the dark from the next street, killing him. Panic quickly overflows—the rate of cutting predictably increasing, the angles tilting to either side to suggest the gathering collective madness—as the lights in different houses and cars begin to flash on and off.

J. P. Telotte describes the change in the neighborhood "as if the normal world of Andy Hardy's town had suddenly become a scene from a film noir" (12)—a most appropriate description given that Maple Street is actually the old set for Andy Hardy's Midwestern town of Carvel. Serling's writing for the episode was clearly influenced by Frank Capra's classic *It's a Wonderful Life* (1946), in which we also see an archetypal American town turned into a noirish nightmare when the guardian angel Clarence shows our hero George Bailey (James Stewart) what life would be like if he hadn't existed. (*It's a Wonderful Life* is invoked by a number of other *Twilight Zone* episodes including "A Passage for Trumpet" [1.32: May 20, 1960], "Mr. Bevis" [1.33: June 6, 1960], and "A Hundred Yards over the Rim.") At the end of "Maple Street" there is a cut to an extreme long shot as we see the two aliens who have engineered the strange events looking down from a high vantage point on the street, where the neighbors have turned into a self-destructive mob. One alien explains to the other that humans are "their worst enemy" when frightened. "Throw them into darkness for a few hours and then, sit back and watch the pattern," the alien concludes; it's always the same because "the world is full of Maple Streets."

Presnell and McGee are relatively charitable in their assessment of "Maple Street," seeing it as nothing less than a "capsule 1950s American history lesson" (55) of Cold War anxieties. Rick Worland, though, views the episode as ideologically conflicted. For him, the problem is the twist ending, where it is revealed that the aliens are real, not just the paranoid imagination of the average folk of Maple Street. Therefore, he argues that the story initially shows a typically pleasant American community that is only a thin veneer hiding paranoia and hatred, and it seemingly condemns these attitudes but then "pulls back to reestablish 'normality' for the viewer as the Cold War status quo, the implacable enemy at our doorstep against whom we must unite before it's too late" (106).

Similar concerns are voiced by Erik Mortenson, who argues that the anxieties aroused and addressed by the pilot episode, "Where Is Everybody?" (aired as the first episode on Friday, October 2, 1959), are negated or recuperated by "placing it within a patriotic theme of American space exploration" (67). In the plot, Mike Ferris (Earl Holliman) finds himself inexplicably alone in a strangely abandoned town, suffering from apparent amnesia. He knows he is an American, although, as he says, "there's some question about my identity. I'm not sure who I am." For Mortenson, the episode is "a comment not only on the human condition in general, but on the specific postwar anxiety about isolation fostered by the move to the suburbs and the relentless striving of the executive in his 'grey flannel suit'" (62). Indeed, "The place is here, the time is now," observes Serling in his opening voice-over, "and the journey into the shadows that we're about to watch could be our journey." The celestial stars of the show's famous title graphic dissolve into the shot of a bland, sunless sky, setting the episode's stark and unremitting tone; in changing from a fantastical drawing to the photographically real, the dissolve encapsulates the intent of the series as a whole—to deliver viewers to the world of the fantastic, "out there," and then to bring them back down to earth, to the here and now.

Ferris (we learn his name only at the end) wanders about the town of Oakwood, his panic growing as he tries to find other people and figure out what's going on. The doors to all the shops on Main Street are open but no one is to be seen anywhere. Talking to himself, Ferris finally remembers that he is in the Air Force but little more. He begins to go mad, the blankly staring eye of an optometrist's sign seeming to signal a godless or at least an indifferent world, as in F. Scott Fitzgerald's *The Great Gatsby* (1925). With quick cuts the shots alternate between close-ups of Ferris and of blinking traffic lights, the blinking and rapid editing indicative of the man's rising panic, the tilted angles expressing his loss of mental stability. In the end of "Where Is Everybody?" it is revealed that what we are seeing is actually Ferris's nightmarish mental breakdown while being tested in extended isolation by the military in preparation for enduring the psychological demands that future space travel will involve.

In his nightmare, Ferris wonders "Did they drop the bomb?" The dialogue requires no exposition about which bomb he is referring to or what its dropping might mean, for the audience already knows full well. The space race was on: in the same month that "Where Is Everybody?" aired, the first ICBMs with nuclear warheads were deployed by the US military and the Russian Lunik 3 probe took the first pictures of the far side of the moon. With its uninhabited town, the episode taps into fantasies of nuclear apocalypse (in the "Oakwood" drugstore, all the paperbacks in the display rack are filled with the same book, *The Last Man on Earth*) exploited in such postwar science-fiction movies as *Five* (1951), *Robot Monster* (1953), *Day the World Ended* (1955) and *The World, the Flesh, and the Devil* (1959), the latter released the same year as *The Twilight Zone* began with this episode.

Douglas Sirk's *Battle Hymn* (1957), conspicuously announced on the marquee and on lobby posters at the "Oakwood" cinema, is perhaps a deliberate choice for the sake of contrast, for if Sirk's film presents idealized images in ravishing Technicolor (however ironic critics subsequently may have found them to be),* *The Twilight Zone*, although equally expressionistic in black and white with tight, sweaty close-ups of Ferris's face, stands in stark visual opposition to it. (Surely some of Serling's own experiences as a paratrooper in World War II, where he suffered a shrapnel wound and likely PTSD as well, informed his writing for this opening episode and for several others featuring combat-related situations.) Nevertheless, as Mortenson argues, "Where Is Everybody?" ultimately comes down fully in support of America's space efforts. As Ferris is being carried out of the lab on a stretcher and is asked what happened to him, he says, understandably, that he was in "a place I don't want to go again." Still, the general in charge (James Gregory) insists that the experiment was a success, a

* See, for example, Laura Mulvey and John Halliday, eds., *Douglas Sirk* (London: Edinburgh Film Festival, 1972), and Barbara Klinger, *Melodrama and Meaning: History, Culture, and the Films of Douglas Sirk* (Bloomington and Indianapolis: Indiana University Press, 1994).

small step for man but a giant step for mankind. Even Ferris, supine on his stretcher, despite his previous remark about not wanting to return, is quickly able to regain his senses before being placed in the ambulance, look skyward, and ask the moon to wait for him because, like General MacArthur, he'll be back ("Next time it won't be a dream or a nightmare, next time it'll be for real"), after which the moon dissolves into the stars of the familiar *Twilight Zone* title graphic as the episode ends.

Similarly, there is no question about the pro-American stance of "A Hundred Yards over the Rim," a time-travel story that begins in the New Mexico desert in 1847 with a small party of parched pioneers desperately in need of water. Just as the band decides to turn back, one of the men, Christian Horn (Cliff Robertson), frantic to find water for his sick son, leaves the wagons to go over one last rise. To his amazement, he finds a paved highway

Mike Ferris (Earl Holliman) wondering "Where Is Everybody?"

with trucks and cars, having somehow been transported to the future (our present). He comes to a diner, where the owner's wife, Mary Lou (Evans Evans), gives him some penicillin with which he flees from the police back over the rim to give to his son. Finding his family and the others where he apparently had left them just a moment ago, Horn rhapsodizes to his fellow pioneers with a distant look in his eye about the progress the future will bring to the desert: "There'll be highways and many new things. A whole new land . . . It was people like us. We made it happen." His celebration of "progress" elides the settler history of the nation and its genocide of Native American peoples, like the classic Hollywood Western the show frequently invokes, and is undergirded with an implicit endorsement of Manifest Destiny. There is no irony to the episode, either stylistically or in the ending; clearly, God is on America's side if He allows for such miracles in order to save worthy white folk who will help advance westward the course of empire.

Telotte sees the series' typical ending, as in "Maple Street," in which the camera pulls away to a more distant vantage point (eventually, usually, back to the sky where the episode began) as articulating a sense of viewers "recoiling" from an uncomfortable world "to regain the distance at which they began their narrative experience" (Telotte, 14). He argues that this brings comfortable closure to otherwise disturbing material, but it may also be argued that it is precisely this "withdrawal" that allows viewers to consider with greater knowledge the follies and mistakes of the characters they have been watching—to, as it were, recollect in relative tranquility. Plantinga makes a similar argument regarding those "frame shifter" endings. This dynamic recalls Scholes's argument, noted earlier, regarding speculative fiction, echoed by Darko Suvin's famous understanding of science fiction as working by providing us with an experience of "cognitive estrangement."

This effect is literalized in the end of "Maple Street" as we watch the aliens watching what they have wrought from a distance.

In those final shots the panicked humans running madly in the street look like insects in a controlled experiment—not unlike the way the commander of the rescue ship describes Benteen's isolated society in "On Thursday We Leave for Home." But crucially, in "Maple Street," when the camera pulls back, we see not only the frightened denizens of Maple Street as they destroy each other, but also, we observe the alien observers from behind. Thus, we see more than both the average people of Maple Street and even more than the alien invaders do. The viewer's identification with the townspeople is ruptured even earlier: before Charlie shoots at the unknown intruder, a close-up shows the hammer in the approaching figure's tool belt, revealing it to be Pete, who was shown doing carpentry at the beginning. Hence, we are positioned to judge Charlie's actions as rash, dangerous, wrong. At the end, the first line of alien dialogue as the camera positions itself behind them is "Understand the procedure now?"—which might just as well be addressed to the episode's more enlightened viewers now that they have witnessed the debacle unfolding on Main Street.

David Melbye notes that not all episodes of *The Twilight Zone* have twist endings, but "any *Twilight Zone* episode's narrative resolution is less necessarily oriented around shock and surprise than correcting moral imbalances" (192). This moral emphasis is key to the show and might be described as a vague humanism characterized by lofty social ideals that individual behavior usually belied. Perhaps the worst sin for Serling is a disdain for other people, for not considering the common good, as manifest in the extreme by the likes of Oliver Crangle (Theodore Bikel) in "Four O'Clock" or the Chancellor (Fritz Weaver) in "The Obsolete Man." We know that Franklin Gibbs (Everett Sloan) is gripped by "the fever" in the eponymous episode when he snaps at his wife (Vivi Janiss), "The devil with people. I'm not concerned with people." At the same time, the state, for Serling, must respect and accommodate the needs of the individuals of which it is comprised. At the end of "The

The viewer sees more than the aliens at the end of "The Monsters Are Due on Maple Street."

Obsolete Man," written by Serling, when the chancellor of a future totalitarian society in which religion and books have been deemed "obsolete" and banned is himself judged obsolete and sentenced to death, Serling seems momentarily to step out of his wry persona and to speak from his heart when he asserts that "any state, any entity, any ideology that fails to recognize the worth, the dignity, the rights of man, that state is obsolete. A case to be filed under 'M' for mankind—in the Twilight Zone."

One political science professor has offered an extended exegesis subtitled "The Political Theory of Rod Serling," arguing that Serling's predominantly negative view of human nature derives from political philosopher Thomas Hobbes's famous account of the social world as one of "war of all against all" (Feldman). Thus, as Dr. Stockton observes at the end of "The Shelter," his neighbors had become like "naked, wild animals" fighting for their own survival. The scene of the card game in "The Trade-Ins" (3.31: April 20, 1962) in which the gambler Farraday (Theo Marcuse) folds a winning hand and allows the desperate John Holt (Joseph Schildkraut), an obviously easy mark, to leave with his own money is so poignant precisely because it is an act of selfless kindness quite different from the way people usually behave on *The Twilight Zone*. Serling emphasizes the singular nature of Farraday's generous gesture in his final remark that the episode is offered as "a reminder from all the sentimentalists in the Twilight Zone."

In that final interview before his death, Serling described his relationship with producers as a Hobbesian one of "adversaries": "When all the smoke clears and the ozone lifts, your enemy is the producer, that's the guy you're competing with, and you have to battle him, just as if you were an adversary" (Brevelle). Boxing, which figures in "The Big Tall Wish" and "Steel" (as well as providing the setting for *Requiem for a Heavyweight*), offers a fundamental Hobbesian metaphor of man against man. The episodes in which men in the desert turn on and kill each other ("I Shot an Arrow," "The Rip Van Winkle Caper") also are, like the famous Death Valley climax in Erich von Stroheim's *Greed* (1924), elemental visualizations of this dark view of human nature. In "I Shot an Arrow," the commander of the crashed ship, Col. Donlin (Edward Binns), tries—unsuccessfully—to maintain "protocol" and to operate "by the book," but the inherent selfishness of men in the struggle to survive makes that impossible.

There is, certainly, an "individualist ideology that permeates the series" (Booker, 58). "On Thursday We Leave for Home" makes clear Serling's preference for individualism over collectivism: "Now it's time to be what God meant you to be . . . individuals," the ship's commander tells Benteen, who wants to maintain a group lifestyle for his fellow colonists after their return to Earth. But, at the same time, individualism needs constant containment and regulation because people (men, mostly) on *The Twilight Zone* tend to succumb to individual needs and drives, forgetting the common good. Hence, demagogues rear up regularly in the Zone, as in “The Obsolete Man,” “He's Alive,” and “Four O'Clock.” In “The Little People” astronaut Peter Craig (Joe Maross) transforms, as he says, from “a slob with a slide rule to—a God” when he discovers a miniature society on an alien world that as a giant by comparison he can rule with absolute power.

How, then, to keep this will to power in check? In “The Man in the Bottle” (2.2: October 7, 1960) a modest shopkeeper, Arthur Castle (Luther Adler), discovers a genie (Joseph Ruskin) in one of his curios. Initially content in life, the prospect of having four (!) wishes soon sparks his egomania. When Castle wishes for power, he finds himself as Hitler in his *Führerbunker* before committing suicide. He gets the point and so uses his final wish to be himself again, learning from the experience to be more accepting of his place in life. The episode ends with him and his wife laughing, with everything back to the way it was (down to the crack in the shop display case that was repaired with the first wish), as in a traditional sitcom. “You take what you get, and you live with it,” as the jazz musician Joey Crown (Jack Klugman) observes in “A Passage for Trumpet.” Serling tells us explicitly at the end of “Once upon a Time” “that there is much wisdom” in the phrase ‘Stay in your own backyard.’ To which it might be added, ‘and if possible, assist others to stay in theirs.’

Whether the result of divine order, supernatural agency, alien intervention, or happenstance, the status quo is often reinstated on *The Twilight Zone*, the state of affairs literally returning to the way things were before. In “The Prime Mover” (2.21: March 24, 1961), for example, a cook in a dinner, Jimbo Cobb (Buddy Ebsen), possesses the power of telekinesis. His partner, Ace Larsen (Dane Clark), discovers his secret and takes the reluctant Jimbo to Las Vegas, where they go on a winning gambling spree using his mental ability to turn the dice in their favor. But because he regards using his power as cheating, hence unethical, Jimbo opts to forego the temptations of wealth and return to his dreary blue-collar job even as Ace is increasingly blinded by visions of wealth and its material benefits. Similarly, in the future envisioned in "The Trade-Ins" an elderly couple, John and Marie Holt (Alma Platt), look to avail themselves of a commercial service whereby they can transplant their minds into young, healthy bodies. They only have enough money for one of them to have the procedure, which John reluctantly agrees to do because he is seriously ill and in constant pain. Afterward, he revels in his new body's physical abilities, but in the end the couple decides that the new age difference between them is too wide a gap, and John opts to return to his original body so that they may spend their remaining time together as they would naturally.

Jimbo Cobb and John Holt choose to return to their previous existences, but all those *Twilight Zone* characters with the moral flaws of greed, selfishness, and cynicism who try to get ahead dishonestly in the end receive, like George Minafer in *The Magnificent Ambersons* (1942), their comeuppance. As Serling says at the end of "Sounds and Silences" of the pompous Roswell G. Flemington (John McGiver), a tyrannical armchair sea captain now hoisted on his own yardarm, "All Mr. Flemington is suffering from is a case of poetic justice." At the end of "A Kind of a Stopwatch," in which boorish loudmouth Patrick McNulty ends up in a world frozen in time with no one to talk to, Serling pronounces that "now he's just been handed the bill." Just as justice, even if it is sometimes particularly cruel ("That's not fair!" cries Bemis correctly at the end of "Time Enough at Last"), grim ("Elegy"), or ironic ("Escape Clause"), the implication is that the universe eventually sets things aright. At the end of "Execution," in which the nineteenth-century murderous cowboy is murdered in the present and his killer dies in the noose meant for him in the past, Serling observes that the story demonstrates that "justice can span years. Retribution is not subject to a calendar." He quotes Shakespeare's *Hamlet* at the end of "The Last Flight" (1.18: February 5, 1960) to the effect that there is more to the universe than imagined by our philosophy; nevertheless, the order of things as designed by the divine watchmaker is very much like a familiar combination of the American legal system and standard institutional bureaucracy.

Meting out this divine justice consistently on *The Twilight Zone* is a regulated and finely tuned network with its own rules and regulations. In "One for the Angels" when we first see Mr. Death (Murray Hamilton) he is busily jotting information in a notepad, keeping his records in order. Pip (Sebastian Cabot), Rocky Valentine's guide to "the other place" after he dies in "A Nice Place to Visit," also keeps information on his assignee in a notepad. Later Valentine goes to check his personal file in the "Hall of Records," which is a supernatural-looking stairway with rows of mundane filing cabinets on it. Mr. Death in "One for the Angels" is eager to get down to "business" because "we have to keep these things efficient" and keep to the "timetable." Explaining to Bookman (Ed Wynne) that he should prepare for his "departure" that evening, Mr. Death provides details on the three main categories of appeals: hardship cases (surviving spouse or children), priority cases (the person is on the verge of an important discovery, for example), and "unfinished business of a major nature," which Bookman invokes as a stalling tactic. Similarly, in "Escape Clause" the devil, Mr. Cadwallader (Thomas Gomez) explains that the titular escape clause is article 99 in his contract, which must be invoked for requesting "departure." In "A Game of Pool" the best billiards player waits in limbo until being called to meet a challenge over a loudspeaker, implying a heavenly headquarters with electricians and dispatcher.

Toward the end of "Cavender Is Coming" the camera pans up from the hapless Agnes Grepp (Carol Burnett) to her guardian angel (Jesse White) through the very same painted star-filled sky that appears in the show's opening to a heavenly office door

The Hall of Records in "A Nice Place to Visit."

marked "Third Celestial Division, Angel Placement." In the show, most of the characters who encounter this bureaucracy from the beyond seek to finesse its rules but ultimately accept its determinations, even unto death, like Bookman in "One for the Angels." At the end of that episode, as the old salesman now goes off willingly with Mr. Death, Bookman pauses to wonder where he's going: "Up there?" he nervously asks. "You made it!" Mr. Death reassures this exceedingly nice fellow (and viewers as well) that he will be justly rewarded in the afterlife for his behavior in this one. Noël Carroll identifies what he calls "Tales of Dread" in *The Twilight Zone*, those episodes in which there seems to be a guiding force or intelligence in the universe, arguing that they are indicative of paranoid thinking and that they induce anxiety and dread because we fear retribution from beyond if we morally transgress in some way (31–33). But one might equally argue the opposite, that such a vision is comforting rather than unsettling because it mirrored postwar American society and implied a system continuous with it even in the afterlife.

Often, Serling's closing comments reinforced this sense of an efficient celestial force policing the universe by referring to the Zone's elaborate information archive: "You might check under 'B' for baseball in the Twilight Zone" ("The Mighty Casey"), "Look for it filed under 'M' for machines . . . in the Twilight Zone" ("A Thing about Machines" [2.4: October 28, 1960]), "A case to be filed under 'M' for mankind . . . in the Twilight Zone" ("The Obsolete Man"), and so on. At the end of "A Game of Pool" Serling acknowledges that there are "ground rules" even in the Twilight Zone. *The Twilight Zone* thus provoked and reassured audiences at the same time, disturbing viewers with revelations of forces beyond human understanding but also reassuring them with their quotidian familiarity, a tangled and complex but usually fair bureaucracy duplicating that of postwar America. A show that challenged viewers to open themselves to new possibilities and alternatives to the way things are, it also depicted those alternatives in familiar ways that endorsed and naturalized the status quo. By "taming" the fantastic in this way, *The Twilight Zone* was able to present socially conscious drama without alienating "the lady in Dubuque"—precisely the "mass taste" Serling had thought possible to achieve.

Along with this tension between the fantastic and the familiar in *The Twilight Zone* is the political tension or paradox that informs its moral vision. A show that espoused liberal sentiments regarding democracy and individualism, *The Twilight Zone*, as already indicated, also viewed human nature as dangerous, driven largely by greed, self-interest, and a will to power. This thematic tension at the heart of the show places it squarely within the debates that have informed American culture and political thought from the nation's beginning. The work of Thomas Hobbes was influential on the political thinking of the

Founding Fathers. John Adams, quoting Machiavelli, wrote, for example, "That whoever would found a state and make proper laws for the government of it must presume that all men are bad by nature: that they will not fail to show that natural depravity of heart whenever they have a fair opportunity" (IV: 408). Political philosophers who followed Hobbes, even if they disagreed with his view of human nature as primally brutal and selfish, nonetheless conceded that there was a difference between the individual man as he would be in the hypothetical state of nature and as he actually existed in society and, moreover, that his "innate depravity" was encouraged by a democratic political system. As Alexis de Tocqueville, perhaps the most perceptive of Europeans to visit the nascent American republic, famously observed, "Aristocracy links everybody, from peasant to king, in one long chain. Democracy breaks the chain and frees each link" (II: 478). Ever since Hobbes, political thinkers espousing democratic principles have theorized how to bind those links for the good of both individuals and society at large. With *The Twilight Zone*, Rod Serling joined the ranks of such otherwise very different American artists as Walt Whitman, Frank Capra, and Frederick Wiseman, all of whom have sought in their work to find ways to integrate the individual within the great democratic project of the nation.

Zoning Out

100 Serling reminded his audience every week that the Twilight Zone is, after all, "a dimension not only of sight and sound, but of mind." As I've suggested, we might interpret this to refer to the tension between the televisual medium as commercial spectacle on the one hand ("sight and sound") and as socially conscious art ("mind") on the other and to refer to *The Twilight Zone* itself as a battleground where this conflict was waged. Serling's uneasy relationship with sponsors and the formulaic nature of commercial television, which he at once resisted and exploited, is evident in *The Twilight Zone*, a show that reveals the tensions between artistic ambition and commercial capitulation at a pivotal point in the history of the medium. Like Serling himself, *The Twilight Zone* was caught in a twilight zone, a liminal "middle ground" between opposing forces.

Serling remained ambivalent about the medium of television. In 1956 he said that "of all the media, TV lends itself most beautifully to presenting a controversy. You can just take part of a controversy and, using just a small number of people, get your point across"; four years later he wrote that "the half-hour film has always been an imitative, doggy, telegraphed, insipid, assembly-line product since its inception eleven years ago" (qtd. in Boddy 1984, 100–101). According to William Boddy, Serling alternately depicted his work on the show "as a capitulation in his struggles as industry reformer or the logical outcome of his battles for serious television drama" (105). Perhaps this ambivalence was inevitable given Serling's ambitions just at the crossroads of the medium's transition from the period of live anthology drama to the more standardized series format.

In one of the series' last episodes, "What's in the Box," the home TV of taxi driver Joe Britt (William Demerest) plays his own unhappy life story, including his future, which then advances into the near future to show him killing his wife in a domestic rage. Of course, trying to prevent the tragedy from becoming a reality, Britt causes it to happen. Serling introduces the episode by saying, "Mr. Britt is going to watch a really big shew" in the manner of Ed Sullivan—an intertextual reference to the extremely popular Sunday-night variety show (CBS, 1948–71) that newspaper-columnist Sullivan hosted for many years on "most of these same stations." In the *Twilight Zone* episode, a doctor (Herbert Lytton) diagnoses Britt as being bewildered about distinguishing between reality and illusion because of his immersion in the atemporal flow of television. The doctor concludes that Britt is suffering from a delusion brought about by being a TV addict, apparently lured into the vast wasteland by identifying too much with the characters in the shows he watches. Television has turned his mind to "oatmeal," as Ed Lindsay had prophesized in "Static."

Nevertheless, Serling remained adamant that, as he told Mike Wallace, "this is my medium and I understand it. I'm a dramatist for television. This is the area I know. I've been trained for it." With *The Twilight Zone* he perfected the structure of the half-hour "semi-anthology drama" (Kraszewski, 348), dangling an opening hook with a fantastic premise, expanding upon that premise for two acts with a new hook in the middle before the commercial break, and then following with the twist and denouement ("whoosh, up over, and whammo!" as Carling

[Edward Andrews] blithely describes atomic war in "Third from the Sun"). As Gary Hoppenstand observes, *The Twilight Zone* demonstrates that Rod Serling "fully understood the potential of the television medium" (562).

Certainly, Serling's awareness of the televisual medium suffused *The Twilight Zone* like the shifting fog in the series' original opening. Already in the pilot episode, "Where Is Everybody?," the presence of television is significant, as Ferris is secretly being monitored by scientists on closed-circuit TV throughout his isolation ordeal. In other episodes television is similarly associated with surveillance and the dark side of technology. "Black Leather Jackets" offers a visual joke about *The Twilight Zone*'s own network: the one-eye logo of the intergalactic television sets through which the advance scouts of the alien invasion force communicate resembles the logo of CBS. The role of television in the fascist future of "The Obsolete Man" is significant and complex: on the one hand, it provides a propaganda outlet for the state, as it does in "Eye of the Beholder," while on the other, it permits a form of resistance when the appropriately named librarian Wordsworth (Burgess Meredith) entraps the Chancellor into imploring an "obsolete" God to spare him during Wordsworth's own televised death (hints of the first *Black Mirror* episode, "The National Anthem" [2011], here). Television also figures prominently in "A Thing About Machines," about Bartlett Finchley (Richard Haydn), a man who despises everything mechanical and then suffers the wrath of his household appliances and devices, including the performer on his television screen, who speaks to him directly. In his introduction to the episode, Serling appears inside a television screen from where he introduces us to Finchley, "a malcontent, born either too late or too early in the century" and then adds tantalizingly, "and who in just a moment will enter a realm where muscles and the will to fight back are not limited to human beings. Next stop for Mr. Bartlett Finchley—the Twilight Zone." On this television screen inside a console, speaking of a character who loses a battle against modernity and the mechanical, we may think of Serling as immersed in the medium or a prisoner of it, the image's ambiguity consistent with his ambivalence toward the medium.

Serling survived the transition from the period of live anthology drama to the telefilm series, taking from live television drama its "small casts and modest sets" and its reliance on medium shots and close-ups while lacking "the typical series' convention of continuing characters and settings" and the "loosely-plotted narrative structures" of the series format (Boddy 1984, 101, 107). But after five seasons of *The Twilight Zone*, Serling's best work was behind him. Already the final two seasons betrayed a decided falling off of overall quality, with episodes, especially those written by Serling, recycling ideas used earlier: "He's Alive," for example, revisits ideas from "Death's-Head Revisited," while "No Time Like the Past" (4.10: March 7, 1963) reworks "Back There."

By the time the fourth season began in January, Serling had spent the fall semester teaching writing and mass media at Antioch College, and although he would continue writing for the show, he became less involved in the details of production (Zicree, 293). He was already working on the screenplay for *Seven Days in May* (1964), the film version of the 1962 best-selling thriller by Fletcher Knebel and Charles W. Bailey II about an attempted military coup of the American government led by a charismatic, self-righteous general who perceives the president as soft on Communism. The novel was perfectly suited to Serling's sensibility—which is perhaps why the screenplay is so faithful to its source and the best screenplay Serling managed to produce for film. Like the movie based on it, the novel concludes with an explicit civics lesson, one to which it has been building all along: as we learn what each of the various characters is doing now that the coup has been thwarted, all are listening in different places to the president's speech to the nation extolling the democratic process and the ongoing civic responsibilities it requires as he prepares to go abroad to negotiate a possible but contentious disarmament treaty with the Soviet Union: "Once the President and the Senate, as the responsible authorities, make a decision, then, my fellow citizens, debate and opposition among the military must come to an end . . . Any other way would mean confusion, chaos and certain defeat" (354). The film, directed by John Frankenheimer (who had directed Serling's script for "A Town Has Turned to Dust," with its similarly civic-minded theme), preserves the scene, with the president's speech about responsible democratic citizenship conveniently providing the pedestal that Serling otherwise no doubt would have erected himself to remind the public about the ethics of individualism in a democratic society.

Five years after the end of *The Twilight Zone* Serling returned as host of *Night Gallery* for three seasons. Episodes of the ninety-minute weekly anthology series featured Serling in an art gallery space introducing each story in front of a usually slapdash painting minimally related to it. Serling contributed a number of scripts to the show, some original and some adaptations, but unlike the situation with *The Twilight Zone*, he had no creative control over *Night Gallery*. Nevertheless, Stephen King's blunt assessment that it was "really a watered-down *Thriller* with Serling doing the Boris Karloff hosting job" (King, 234) may be somewhat harsh. (Among its more noteworthy moments is the segment "Eyes" starring Joan Crawford from the pilot episode, which was Steven Spielberg's first professional credit as director). Yet, however we might assess the quality of *Night Gallery* now, Serling's presence alone was sufficient to provide the show with a patina of the weird.

Rod Serling was only fifty when he died in 1975 from complications following surgery after a heart attack, no doubt brought on by his heavy smoking and chronic fatigue from his intense work schedule. *The Twilight Zone*, his greatest achievement, stood out as a beacon of cathode light, thoughtful and artfully crafted, amid the darkness of that vast televisual wasteland. Unlike any television show before it, it addressed the anxieties of the age with tightly constructed fantastic fables that sought to engage viewers reflectively through both content and construction. If its promise of a "wondrous land whose boundaries are that of the imagination" was ultimately another place circumscribed by dominant liberal values, the show could hardly be faulted given its context of network television at a pivotal moment in its history.

This is by no means to suggest, however, that *The Twilight Zone* is only of interest today for its historical significance. If that were so, we could not account for the show's pervasive and continuing presence in popular culture, as chronicled at the beginning of this book. Serling observed in his last interview in 1975 that "there's no room" anymore for a show like *The Twilight Zone* with its speculative parables because "the problems are so much with us that they have to be attacked directly" (Brevelle) rather than metaphorically. Certainly, no other mainstream television shows since have succeeded in reflecting the contemporary zeitgeist as memorably. But if there is any doubt that the show remains as relevant today, in the era of the Trump presidency, as it was in its time, let us return one last time to "The Monsters Are Due on Maple Street." Serling concludes the episode by commenting that:

> The tools of conquest do not necessarily come with bombs and explosions and fallout. There are weapons that are simply thoughts, attitudes, prejudices—to be found only in the minds of men. For the record, prejudices can kill and suspicion can destroy, and a thoughtless, frightened search for a scapegoat has a fallout all its own—for the children, and the children yet unborn. And the pity of it is that these things cannot be confined to "The Twilight Zone."

Submitted for your consideration.

REFERENCES

Adams, John. *The Works of John Adams, Second President of the United States: With a Life of the Author, Notes and Illustrations by his Grandson Charles Francis Adams*. Edited by Charles Frances Adams. 10 vols. Boston: Little, Brown and Co., 1856. https://oll.libertyfund.org/2098.

Alloway, Lawrence. *Violent America: The Movies, 1946–1964*. New York: Museum of Modern Art, 1971.

Astruc, Alexandre. "The Birth of a New Avant-Garde: La Caméra Stylo," in *The New Wave*, edited by Peter Graham, 17–23. Garden City, NY: Doubleday, 1968.

Bazin, André. *What Is Cinema?* Vol. 2. Berkeley: University of California Press, 1971.

Beaumont, Charles. *The Twilight Zone Scripts of Charles Beaumont*. Edited by Roger Anker. Colorado Springs: Gauntlet Press, 2004.

Boddy, William. "Entering *The Twilight Zone*." *Screen* 25, nos. 4–5 (July/October 1984): 98–108.

———. *Fifties Television: The Industry and Its Critics*. Urbana and Chicago: University of Illinois Press, 1990.

Booker, M. Keith. "*The Twilight Zone* and American Society in the Long 1950s: Between the Modern and the Postmodern." In *Strange TV: Innovative Television Series from the Twilight Zone to The X-Files*, edited by M. Keith Booker, 49–70. Westport, CT: Greenwood Press, 2002.

Boulle, Pierre. *Planet of the Apes*. Translated by Xan Fielding. New York: Signet, 1964.

Brevelle, Linda. "Rod Serling: The Facts of Life." First published 1976 in *Writer's Digest*. https://www.rodserling.com/brevelleint.htm.

Brode, Douglas, and Carol Serling. *Rod Serling and The Twilight Zone: The 50th Anniversary Tribute*. Fort Lee, NJ: Barricade Books, 2009.

Carroll, Noël. "Tales of Dread in *The Twilight Zone*: A Contribution to Narratology," in *Philosophy and the Twilight Zone*, edited by Noël Carroll and Lester H. Hunt, 26–38. Malden, MA: Wiley-Blackwell, 2009.

Engel, Joel. *Rod Serling: The Dreams and Nightmares of Life in the Twilight Zone: A Biography*. Chicago: Contemporary Books, 1989.

Feldman, Leslie Dale. *Spaceships and Politics: The Political Theory of Rod Serling*. Plymouth, UK: Lexington Books, 2010.

Fiddy, Dick. "Another Dimension." *Sight and Sound*, January 2018, 62–65.

Grams, Martin Jr. *The Twilight Zone: Unlocking the Door to a Television Classic*. Churchville, MD: OTR Publishing, 2008.

Grant, Barry Keith. *Film Genre: From Iconography to Ideology*. London and New York: Wallflower Press, 2007.

———. *Invasion of the Body Snatchers*. London: British Film Institute, 2010.

Greenberg, Martin Harry, Richard Matheson, and Charles G. Waugh, eds. *The Twilight Zone: The Original Stories*. New York: Avon, 1985.

Gunn, James, ed. *The New Encyclopedia of Science Fiction*. New York: Viking, 1988.

Henry, O. *The Best Short Stories of O. Henry*. Edited by Bennett A. Cerf and Van H. Cartmell. New York: Modern Library, 1944.

Heinlein, Robert A. "Preface to *Tomorrow, The Stars*," 5–10. New York: Doubleday, 1967.

Hey, Kenneth. "*Marty*: Aesthetics vs. Medium in Early Television Drama." In *American History / American Television*, edited by John E. O'Connor, 95–133. New York: Frederick Ungar, 1983.

Hill, Rodney. "Mapping *The Twilight Zone*'s Cultural and Mythical Terrain," in *The Essential Science Fiction Television Reader*, edited by J. P. Telotte, 111–26. Lexington: University of Kentucky Press, 2008.

Hoberman, J. "Camelot Year One: Into the Twilight Zone." In *The Dream Life: Movies, Media, and the Mythology of the Sixties*, 44–54. New York: New Press (Norton), 2003.

Homans, Peter. "Puritanism Revisited: An Analysis of the Contemporary Screen-Image Western." In *Notions of Genre: Writings on Popular Film before Genre Theory*, edited by Barry Keith Grant and Malisa Kurtz, 133–47. Austin: University of Texas Press, 2016.

Hoppenstand, Gary. "Editorial: Television as Metaphor." *Journal of Popular Culture* 37, no. 4 (2004): 561–63.

Houghton, Buck. *What a Producer Does: The Art of Moviemaking (Not the Business)*. New York: Silman-James Press, 1992.

Hunt, Lester H. "'And Now, Rod Serling, Creator of *The Twilight Zone*': The Author as Auteur," in *Philosophy and the Twilight Zone*, edited by Noël Carroll and Lester H. Hunt, 5–25. Malden, MA: Wiley-Blackwell, 2009.

Jackson, Rosemary. *Fantasy: The Literature of Subversion*. New York: Methuen, 1981.

Javna, John. *The Best of Science Fiction TV*. New York: Harmony, 1987.

Jowett, Lorna, and Stacey Abbott. *TV Horror: Investigating the Dark Side of the Small Screen*. London and New York: I. B. Taurus, 2013.

Kawin, Bruce. "Authorship, Design, and Execution," in *Auteurs and Authorship: A Film Reader*, edited by Barry Keith Grant, 190–99. Malden, MA: Blackwell, 2008.

King, Stephen. *Danse Macabre*. New York: Everett House, 1981.

Knight, Damon. *In Search of Wonder*. 2nd ed. Chicago: Advent, 1967.

Knebel, Fletcher, and Charles W. Bailey II. *Seven Days in May*. New York: Bantam, 1962.

Kozloff, Sarah Ruth. "Narrative Theory and Television," in *Channels of Discourse: Television and Contemporary Criticism*, edited by Robert C. Allen, 42–73. Chapel Hill: University of North Carolina Press, 1987.

Laudadio, Nicholas C. "All Manner of Revolving Things: Musical Technology, Domestic Anxiety and *The Twilight Zone*'s 'A Piano in the House.'" *Science Fiction Film and Television* 5, no. 2 (Autumn 2012): 159–76.

Matheson, Richard. *Richard Matheson's* The Twilight Zone *Scripts*. Edited by Stanley Wiater. 2 vols. Colorado Springs: Gauntlet Press, 2001–2002.

Melbye, David. *Irony in* The Twilight Zone*: How the Series Critiqued Postwar American Culture*. Lanham, MD: Rowman and Littlefield, 2016.

Mittell, Jason. *Complex TV: The Poetics of Contemporary Television Storytelling*. New York: New York University Press, 2015.

Mittell, Jason. *Genre and Television: From Cop Shows to Cartoons in American Culture*. New York: Routledge, 2004.

Mortenson, Erik. "A Journey into the Shadows: *The Twilight Zone*'s Visual Critique of the Cold War." *Science Fiction Film and Television* 7, no. 1 (Spring 2014): 55–76.

Moskowitz, Sam. *Seekers of Tomorrow: Masters of Modern Science Fiction*. Westport, CT: Hyperion, 1974.

Murray, Brian. "The Enduring Legacy of *The Twilight Zone*." *New Atlantis*, Winter 2016. https://www.thenewatlantis.com/publications/the-enduring-legacy-of-the-twilight-zone.

Newcomb, Horace. *TV: The Most Popular Art*. Garden City, NY: Anchor Doubleday, 1974.

Norris, Van. "Retro Landscapes: Reorganizing the Frontier in Rod Serling's *The Twilight Zone*," in *Channeling the Future: Essays on Science Fiction and Fantasy Television*, edited by Lincoln Geraghty, 3–23. Lanham, MD: Scarecrow Press, 2009.

Plantinga, Carl. "Frame Shifters: Surprise Endings and Spectator Imagination in *The Twilight Zone*," in *Philosophy and the Twilight Zone*, edited by Noël Carroll and Lester H. Hunt, 39–57. Malden, MA: Wiley-Blackwell, 2009.

Poe, Edgar Allan. "The Philosophy of Composition," in *The Portable Poe*, edited by Philip Van Doren Stern, 549–65. New York: Viking, 1971.

Poe, Edgar Allan. "The Short Story," in *The Portable Poe*, edited by Philip Van Doren Stern, 565–67. New York: Viking, 1971.

Presnell, Don, and Marty McGee. *A Critical History of Television's The Twilight Zone, 1959–1964*. Jefferson, NC: McFarland, 1998.

Scholes, Robert. *Structural Fabulation: An Essay on Fiction of the Future*. Notre Dame, IN: Notre Dame University Press, 1975.

Serling, Carol, ed. *Adventures in The Twilight Zone*. New York: Daw, 1995.

———, ed. *Journeys to The Twilight Zone*. New York: Daw, 1995.

———, ed. *Return to The Twilight Zone*. New York: Daw, 1995.

———, ed. *Twilight Zone: 19 Original Stories on the 50th Anniversary*. New York: Tor, 2009.

Serling, Rod. *As Timeless as Infinity: The Complete* Twilight Zone *Scripts of Rod Serling*. Edited by Tony Alberella. 10 vols. Colorado Springs: Gauntlet Press, 2004–2013.

———. Interview by Mike Wallace. *The Mike Wallace Interview*. 1959. https://archive.org/details/The_Mike_Wallace_Interview___Rod_Serling.

———. *Stories from the Twilight Zone*. New York: Bantam, 1960.

———. *More Stories from the Twilight Zone*. New York: Bantam, 1961.

———. *New Stories from the Twilight Zone*. New York: Bantam, 1962.

———. *The Twilight Zone: Complete Stories*. 3rd ed. New York: TV Books, 1998.

Shattuc, Jane M. "Television Production: Who Makes American TV?" in *A Companion to Television*, edited by Janet Wasko, 142–54. Malden, MA: Blackwell, 2005.

Sirridge, Mary. "The Treachery of the Commonplace." In *Philosophy and the Twilight Zone*, edited by Noël Carroll and Lester H. Hunt, 58–76. Malden, MA: Wiley-Blackwell, 2009.

Stanyard, Stewart T. *Dimensions Behind The Twilight Zone*. Toronto: ECW Press, 2007.

Suvin, Darko. *Metamorphosis of Science Fiction: On the Poetics and History of a Literary Genre*. New Haven: Yale University Press, 1979.

Telotte, J. P. "In the Cinematic Zone of *The Twilight Zone*." *Science Fiction Film and Television* 3, no. 1 (Spring 2010): 1–18.

Tocqueville, Alexis de. *Democracy in America*. Translated by George Lawrence and edited by J. P. Mayer and Max Lerner. New York: Harper and Row, 1966.

Toffler, Alvin. *Future Shock*. New York: Random House, 1970.

Vidal, Gore. "Who Makes the Movies?" in *Auteurs and Authorship: A Film Reader*, edited by Barry Keith Grant, 148–57. Boston: Blackwell, 2008.

Williams, Raymond. *Television: Technology and Cultural Form*. 3rd ed. London: Routledge, 2004.

Wissner, Reba A. "No Time Like the Past: Hearing Nostalgia in *The Twilight Zone*." *Journal of Popular Television* 6, no. 1 (2018): 59–80.

Wood, Robin. "An Introduction to the American Horror Film," in *American Nightmare: Essays on the Horror Film*, edited by Richard Lippe and Robin Wood, 7–28. Toronto: Festival of Festivals, 1979.

Worland, Rick. "Sign-Posts up Ahead: *The Twilight Zone*, *The Outer Limits*, and TV Political Fantasy 1959–1965." *Science Fiction Studies* 23, no. 1 (March 1996): 103–23.

Wright, Gene. *Horrorshows: The A-Z of Horror in Film, TV, Radio and Theatre*. New York: Facts on File, 1986.

Zicree, Marc Scott. *The Twilight Zone Companion*. New York: Bantam, 1982.

INDEX

Page numbers in boldface refer to illustrations.

ABOUT THE AUTHOR

BARRY KEITH GRANT is professor emeritus of film and popular culture at Brock University, Ontario, Canada. He is the author or editor of many books, including *Shadows of Doubt: Negotiations of Masculinity in American Genre Films* (Wayne State University Press, 2010) and *Documenting the Documentary: Close Readings of Documentary Film and Video*, co-edited with Jeannette Sloniowski (Wayne State University Press, 2013). An Elected Fellow of the Royal Society of Canada, his work has appeared in numerous journals and anthologies and has been translated into several languages.

CPSIA information can be obtained
at www.ICGtesting.com
Printed in the USA
BVHW042156100220
571984BV00010B/128

9 780814 345788